A Countryman's Year

I like the hunting of the hare
Better than that of the fox;
I like the joyous morning air
And the crowing of the cocks.

I like the calm of the early fields,
The ducks asleep by the lake,
The quiet hour which Nature yields
Before mankind is awake.

I like the pheasants and feeding things
Of the unsuspicious morn.
I like the flap of the woodpigeon's wings
As she rises from the corn.

I like the blackbird's shriek and his rush
From the turnips as I pass by,
And the partridge hiding her head in a bush
For her young ones cannot fly.

I like these things and I like to ride
When all the world is in bed
To the top of the hill where the sky grows wide,
And where the sun grows red.

Wilfred Scawen Blunt
from 'The Old Squire'

A Countryman's Year

JOHN HUMPHREYS

Illustrated by John Paley

DAVID & CHARLES

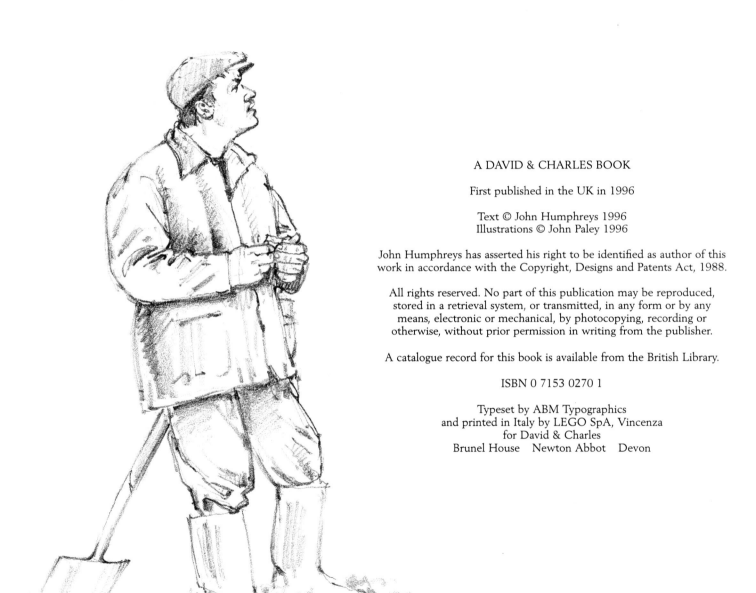

A DAVID & CHARLES BOOK

First published in the UK in 1996

Text © John Humphreys 1996
Illustrations © John Paley 1996

A catalogue record for this book is available from the British Library.

ISBN 0 7153 0270 1

Typeset by ABM Typographics
and printed in Italy by LEGO SpA, Vincenza
for David & Charles
Brunel House   Newton Abbot   Devon

Contents

Foreword

There are not many left of that sturdy breed of village folk who lived in ways little changed for centuries. Times were not easy fifty years ago, with no Welfare State or access to the courts to prop up those who fell on hard times. They learned to survive by resourcefulness, how to make the most of the things they found around them, to eke things out, use them up and make them last.

They kept bees, hens and pigs, tended vegetable patches and in autumn gathered and saved hedge fruit, preserving, pickling and storing, for a cottage with a good supply of logs, salted pork, a potato clamp and jar upon jar of homemade jams and pickles could face the rigours of winter with confidence. Their lot was bound up with the prosperity of the farm and the success of the corn harvest: many of them were directly involved in it.

Some of the menfolk spent a lifetime walking behind horses, forking sheaves, tending the threshing drum and laying hedges. Their children made their hob-nail booted way to the village school every morning. Their wives tended vegetables, darned socks, scrimped and saved and cooked whatever they could glean or garner to hold the family together.

Sometimes they winked at the Game Laws and a rabbit or hare, caught by a method known to the Normans, found its way to a poor man's pot. Some took to the poaching life, others became gamekeepers, but above all they were a community: they hung together. They went to church, rang the bells, bellowed in the choir, enjoyed few simple pleasures but sang, played cricket, danced the valeta and visited the pub when funds permitted. They travelled on foot or bicycle. When they died they went to swell the ranks of the 'rude fore-fathers of the hamlet' who slept their long sleep beneath grassy mounds in the shadow of the church.

This is their story; the page fell open and their earthy figures crept onto it, the fishermen, fowlers, beekeepers, poachers, keepers, bell-ringers, school children, harvesters, thatchers and village cricketers of long ago. Their like could be found in a thousand villages in England. Before the memory of them dies, some of their simple joys and sorrows are recorded in the pages which follow – quickly, ere they fade. Bound up with them are accounts of the rooks, otters, trees, woods and rivers which filled the stage upon which they played out their little lives.

Now their cottages are occupied by new folk with different aspirations enjoying a prosperity undreamed of in the old days. Once there were three cars in the village, now every household boasts at least two. The new folk do not know wheat from barley and perhaps it matters not, for now the corn harvest is irrelevant to all save the farmer. They may be computer-literate but they do not look over bridges or scan the tree-tops to watch the birds. They keep no rusty shotgun in the kitchen, have no ferrets or nets, and no cane angle rod leans by the shed. Their lives are complicated, fast and stressful; they do not go to church and they know no songs. Let a cow pat appear in the High Street, a dog bark or cockerels crow, and they appeal to the courts to remove these nuisances.

What follows is a backward glance at the simple, rugged village people of half a century ago before the old stackyard was filled with neo-Georgian residences and the dame school with computer terminals. These folk have their story and it is worth telling, for from their rustic wisdom and resourcefulness springs much of the character of our island race.

We forget at our peril the old lessons, the old ways and the old people who lived by them

John Humphreys

Bottisham, Cambridgeshire 1996

Dedicated to
Angela, David and Peter

Spring

When it comes the change is barely noticeable. The wind may be just as keen, and the hail as sharp, but a faint stirring tells the countryman that the year is turning. One day is milder than the rest, there is an extra half hour at dusk for outside work, and the first green spears of daffodil bulbs jab up through cottage flowerbeds. Then one day in March there comes a familiar twittering from the heavens and the first martin is here, then a swallow, and our spirits are uplifted by the sight of these tiny messengers come from Africa to nest on the same beam in the cartshed used by their forebears for centuries.

Next comes the mad shout of the cuckoo, cow parsley springs up on the verges, blackbirds nest and the rooks are clamorous in their treetop slums. The gardener sees to his fork and sorts out the seed he husbanded from last year; there is a new bustle in his step.

We are creatures of the sun, we humans, and with the spring comes a quickening of the blood, the sloth of winter falls away and there is a new urgency to be out and about. Summer is not yet here, and a late frost can still catch us unawares, but there is a promise of easier times in the air.

Sable Parliament

I could lie on my back on the truckle bed in my damp and draughty bedroom, one of fourteen in the old vicarage, gaze through the window to where the ancient elms marched between the garden and the churchyard and enjoy drama, domesticity, high jinks, aerobatics, tragedy and courtroom drama. It was before the days of the television which features in the bedrooms of many modern youngsters, for the antics and adventures I witnessed were the real thing. The tops of those elms were home to a great rookery of over a hundred pairs and each March the birds would return to inspect their old nests and assess what maintenance was needed after the winter gales.

They flapped and cawed, renewing pair bonds, quarrelled and started gathering twigs for home repairs. One assiduous pair took turns to fly in, struggling clumsily with a straggly twig which, with great labour, was woven into the fabric of the nest. In their absence a ne'er-do-well from a neighbouring nest would slip across and steal the twig for himself, hauling it out and slipping home with the loot before the householders returned. The sneak burglar was caught in the act and indignant owners gave him a good buffeting which made him mend his ways. The neighbourhood watch scheme was not always effective and there was much cheeky stealing of nesting material by those too idle to forage for themselves.

As the elm buds grew purple and ready to burst, four or five eggs were laid, creamy-white but blotched heavily with black, grey and brown. Tucked down into that deep cup of the nest, made snug with horsehair, moss, old newspaper and sheep's wool, the hen would crouch, her eggs safely beneath her as spring gales buffeted the branches. The male bird was a faithful husband, although there had been cases of bigamy in that twiggy housing estate. Let any bird try to interfere with an established relation-

ship and there would be recriminations, fighting and wild cawing.

Sometimes I climbed the church tower, up creaking ladders past bells which had rung out for many a coronation, through colonies of bats and the owl roost until I stood dizzily high on the battlements, gripping the rough stone with my white knuckles. There below was the ant-like figure of the postman and the patchwork of the green fen stretching out before me and I could look down on the sitting rooks and see just how wisely they had chosen their nesting sites.

Sometimes the birds would hold an assembly with much excited calling, gathered round in earnest and animated debate. First one would caw and then another: sometimes they would all break out together. In the end a judgement was made and some member of the company would be banished for an antisocial act which I could never identify and driven away by the whole mob never to return. Sometimes they would harry the culprit to death.

As the sun rose in pink over the mossy church tower where the barn owls snored, the rooks would fly out to forage over the meadows and drilling. The pouch at the base of that pickaxe beak could hold an unconscionable number of wireworms and slugs, then back they would come, easily at first while sleep lingered but as the day progressed and the sun warmed, their antics became more exuberant. One would drop in from a great height, his wings half-furled, and when he seemed certain to dash himself into the twigs he applied the air-brakes and settled as lightly as thistle-down, looking round with an air of smug satisfaction. Another would swoop round like a sparrowhawk swinging up from below to land on the nest while a third would whiffle down the wind like a flighting mallard.

Their calls varied from raucous cawing to shrieks, croons and cries, some high-pitched, some little more than groans, the whole colony bursting out in a not unpleasing symphony in the evenings and croaking sleepily during the hours of darkness. The hen birds, waiting hungry on their nests, welcomed their spouses, whom they recognised instantly among the throng, with passionate cries which became muffled as they buried their beaks in the husband's food pouch.

As April advanced, the cacophony included high-pitched and unbroken voices, the querulous cries of newly hatched young. Then both parents would be out foraging to keep a growing family in insects. The shuttle service in and out of the rookery became frantic, a great metropolis of departures and arrivals, full of noise and purposeful activity. Sometimes disaster struck with a spring gale and half-fledged rooks tumbled down into the nettles or a whole nest would become detached and I would stand and gape at that barrow load of sticks almost as big as me, a great wreck of some-one's home tumbled onto the aconites.

My mother took in these orphans of the storm, installed them in the wash house and fed them on bread and milk – such fare was good for growing children so it must surely do for rooks. They came to regard her as mother and provider and she could not make a trip down to the washing line or to cut a cabbage without an attendant train of ragged rooklings hopping and flapping after her with imploring squawks. Sometimes they died, for bread and milk lacked the essential nutrients found in a wireworm, but now and then one grew strong enough on the wing to struggle back aloft to rejoin the family.

Who could ask for a better view from a bedroom window? All spring and early summer I was treated to daily episodes in the centuries-old soap opera which was life in the vicarage rookery. However, disaster lurked round the corner, Armageddon, Apocalypse and The Day of Ragnarök all rolled into one. On the second Saturday in May the squire and his friends came with their rook rifles (Holland and Holland made one especially for the job), shotguns and even crossbows to shoot down the young rooks or squabs which, with their scaly feet, clutched at the branches. They were weak on the wing and unlearned of the wicked ways of the world and they sat tamely and allowed themselves to be shot down while their anxious parents wheeled and cawed high above.

The shotguns boomed and the rifles whip-cracked their deadly threnody and scrofulous black bodies thumped down into the white splashed cow parsley below. The rooks were not wasted but made into a traditional countryman's rook pie. Only the breasts and legs were used, cooked with hard-boiled eggs and herbs. The annual rook shoot was a social occasion and the ladies provided a picnic tea and sometimes even joined in the massacre of the innocents. I watched this tragedy, peeping over my window-sill and clutching a tear-stained handkerchief, wincing at every shot, shedding a fresh tear for each victim as down it clattered – a touching scene no doubt but those birds were my friends and I had watched them every day for three months and would watch them again thereafter. Some I recognised as individuals. Little did I think then that one day I would become a shooting man.

As May advanced the leaves burst out and the later squabs, survivors of the first holocaust, were safe and invisible in their green canopy.

The farmers were convinced that they were doing a useful job of pest control. They were sure that that pointed beak was made to dig up their meadow grass, corn, peas and beans, not to mention steal their precious partridge eggs. Old velveteens said that you could not have a good partridge stock and a rookery on the same estate. He intoned this as though the doctrine had been carved in stone and handed down to Moses, but he was only repeating an old myth passed on to him, never questioned, from the old keepers before him.

Certainly rooks will take the odd egg and seed and can do serious damage to maize later in the year, but when digging in the meadow, they pull out only the rotten grass where the cockchafer grubs are lurking. They eat bushels of wireworms in a year and many other destructive insects.

A century and a half ago some farmers in Devon were convinced that rooks were causing their crops to fail. A bounty was offered on every rook destroyed and they all but wiped them out. The result of this madness was that the crops failed completely for the next three years due to an unprecedented plague of insects, which had probably been responsible for the trouble in the first place. The farmers realised their mistake but such a wrong was harder to right than it had been to commit. They embarked on a lengthy and costly process of reintroduction which was only partly successful.

The Magazine of Natural History recorded a freak swarm of locusts which appeared without warning in the Craven area of Shropshire. Rooks flocked in their tens of thousands and mopped up the lot. A sudden and inexplicable plague of caterpillars on Skiddaw was so legion that it threatened to destroy every scrap of greenstuff on the hill. Rooks love high ground in summer and, again, they came from all points of the compass, happened on the feast and polished them off.

Along with other members of the corvid tribe, rooks have been credited with special powers. They will not nest in a tree which is dying, although to all outward signs it appears perfectly healthy. They probably detect a lessening of pliancy in the topmost twigs. They love to build their colonies round the houses of humans and are said to be able to predict the death of the householder. There are recorded cases of this, such as the old lady in a fenland village round whose house the rooks dwelt. They swung high in the morning air at her coming out and cawed drowsily at her window when the moon was young. One day the lady of that old house fell ill and the shadow of death lay upon her. Then the rooks rose high in the sky with a great wheeling clamour under the red September moon and cawed a wild symphony for hours. That night the old lady died and the rooks dwelt about that house no more.

As weather forecasters rooks are more than useful guides as any countryman will know. Rooks spiralling up on some great thermal are a sign of continued good weather. When storms or foul weather threaten they show excitement and great activity, gather in noisy flocks and fly out to roost earlier than usual.

They do not always nest in trees – a pair once built in the weather-vane of St Olave's church in London and another between the wings of the dragon on Bow church. One nested on the mobile weather-vane of the Exchange in Newcastle so that the nest and its occupants turned this way and that with every shift of the wind. A weather-vane seems an appropriate nesting site for such a sagacious weather forecaster.

They appear shaggy-trousered and shapeless as they march about on a stubble, but they are masters of the sky. They turn on their backs in mid-air, forget they are flying and stop to scratch themselves for fleas, plummet in like black peregrines and as well as their undoubted wisdom and sense of community, they enjoy a coarse sense of humour. It seems unnecessary to shoot down this sable bird of the shining furrows, as English as roast beef and Mr Pickwick, Tunnicliffe paintings and Suffolk farm carts, whether or not he likes the occasional partridge-egg omelette. On balance he does more good than harm and the countryside would be poorer without him. He is by no means as black as he is painted but is a gentle creature.

He seems to have fallen on hard times lately. Dutch elm disease took away his favourite nesting trees and he had to look elsewhere. In my old village a dispossessed colony took over a puny spinney of willows down on the marsh. They stuck it out for one year, found it wanting and decamped again, who knows where?

Passing my old home recently I stopped and strolled round remembered haunts, past mossy grave stones and the old sexton's shed. The vicarage had been pulled down long ago, both my father and mother were dead and disease had struck the great elms. Where those shooting parties stood and generations of rooks had reared their broods in those knotty old trees, swaying high above the heads of the resting forefathers of our hamlet, was a disaster far worse than the murderous second Saturday in May. Our trees had not escaped the plague and had either fallen down or been cut off short to truncated, rotting pillars, travesties of their old glory.

Of their late inhabitants, the rooks, companions of distant childhood who had fired in me a love of nature in general and birds in particular, there was not a sign.

The Keeper's Tale

Old Sam was the third generation of his family to wear the velveteens on the great estate. No longer did his lordship insist on the green jacket with brocade and brass buttons and brown bowler hat of grandfather's time. He still had to be smart, mind you, in three-piece suit of Harris tweed, but the uniform of the days when the old King once came to shoot had long gone.

He leaned on the gate to the old rearing field and let his mind drift back to when he started all those years ago. There had been many changes. In the old days there had been a team of eight keepers on the estate and while some land had been sold for building the motorway and to pay off old debts there was still a sizeable chunk and this he managed on his own with the seasonal help of one part-timer. He had a Land Rover whereas grandad went round on Shanks's pony or a horse and trap. The old man did not hold with new-fangled ways. He believed that just as the farmer's foot on the soil was the best fertiliser, the gamekeeper who walked saw a good deal more of what was going on than the one who viewed life from the wrong side of a windscreen.

When Sam started work on the estate he had left the village school with the barest rudiments of an education but a healthy respect for those folk he had been taught were his betters. He became a slave of one of the beat keepers. He spent mind-numbing days which ran into weeks scrubbing clean the hutches used by the broody hens which hatched the pheasant eggs. This was soul-destroying work and when his heart was sick within him he would be dispatched to the village to buy an ounce of shag tobacco for his master, or set, with a 'look sharp about it', to whitewashing the game larder and scrubbing its flagged floor until it gleamed. Anything less than perfection was punished by a smart clip round his ear.

For this he was paid 8s a week rising to 10 on his thirteenth birthday. He gave his wages straight to his mother who allowed him 6d a week to lavish on himself, although a tanner could be made to go a long way in those days. Sometimes they gave him a rabbit, a bag of firewood or some vegetables from the farm so, hard though he felt his lot to be, he knew he was better off than his contemporaries in the nearby mining town who went down the pit the day they left school and in winter rarely saw the sun. At least he was out in the woods and fields.

The keeper's year began after the echoes of the last shots at the end of January had faded and been lost in the covertside. Cage traps were set to capture pheasants which would produce the eggs for the next generation. Daily the keepers went round removing trapped birds, deftly clipping a wing, popping them into a sack and taking them to the old walled garden which served as their aviary. By the time the first daffodils burst there would be 500 or 600 captive birds which needed daily feeding with corn to keep them in good shape for egg production.

At the same time a flock of broody hens was being prepared, kept in the dark and encouraged to sit on clutches of their own or dummy eggs, getting ready to take on new responsibilities. Spare hens were collected from nearby farms and cottage chicken runs, the keeper paying a few pence for the loan and promising that the hen, or one very like it, would be returned when it had served its purpose.

The rearing field was mown and the hutches set in neat lines, every one correct to the inch. Headkeeper Grimes took a pride in seeing his paddock laid out with military precision so there was no weed, no straggly nettle to break the symmetry and every hutch spotless and painted with creosote as though brand new. The hens were installed, each with a string round one leg attached to a cane jabbed in the ground to make sure that it stayed with its own brood and did not wander. Eggs were set beneath them and the month-long spell of incubation began.

Each day the hens were fed and watered and allowed off the nest to stretch their legs. In dry weather the keeper would sprinkle the eggs with water from a watering can for he knew that high humidity at the right times was the key to a good hatching rate. Rarely was the field left unsupervised. Fox snares were set at the gaps in the hedge, for one night visit from 'Charley' could do great damage. He would kill a dozen hens just for the fun of it and frighten many others. It was important that each hutch was kept barred and safe.

The spring held other tasks. This was rabbiting season before the weeds grew tall and the rabbits produced young. Teams of keepers took their ferrets and worked the great warrens in the park and along the hedge bottoms. The tenants approved, for the bunnies made free with their crops while the poor farmer was not allowed to touch one of them. One tenant farmer on a great estate in Norfolk in Victorian times despaired of growing crops to be eaten by his lordship's game. He blew out his brains saying as he did so, 'I die, but the rabbits have killed me'.

Times were more enlightened now and each estate worker and tenant was given a couple of rabbits as small consolation. The bulk of them were sent down to London by train where there was a booming market. Skins and meat were in demand and the keepers were given a bonus when the rabbit crop had been good. Sometimes they shot the conies with a .410, a tiny gun, but in the hands of some of the keepers it was deadly, a bolting rabbit scuttling barely a few steps before being bowled over.

Another task of the spring was to thin out the vermin. In the old and ignorant days this meant any bird with a hooked beak, foxes, stoats, weasels and any creature which was likely so much as to look twice at a game bird egg or chick. In this way many innocent creatures were destroyed. Sam could remember the gamekeeper's gibbet, the long line where any varmint destroyed would be hung and displayed as a testament to the keeper's diligence. Hawks, crows, and owls swung here, their desiccated carcases dry as old paper, fluttering in the wind. The gibbet had long gone and now keepers knew that owls did them no harm and all birds of prey were protected by law, making a comeback to their old strengths without significantly affecting the wild game population.

The trapping line depended on the old gin trap, now outlawed, set in any spot where a rat or stoat might run. These had to be checked each day and Sam was given responsibility for a score of traps of his own with a penny-a-head bonus for each item of vermin he caught. The keeper showed him how to set them, how to spot the likely places round the boles of fallen trees, in gaps in the hedge and in gateways and how important it was that the hands that set the trap were free of the taint of human scent.

Sam would rub his hands in the soil before handling one. He came to recognise the footprints and droppings of all the inhabitants of the wood.

Out on the heathland the partridge keeper would be finding his nests. Rearing partridges on a large scale lay in the future and each nest in the wild had to be hunted out, its position marked on a map and cosseted and protected until the day the eggs hatched. The little grey partridge was everyone's favourite game bird, fearless in defence of its chicks, a constant parent and careful provider. One hen became so tame that Sam could stroke her gently with his finger as she sat on her eggs.

On some estates they were trying what they called the Euston System. This meant removing the clutch of partridge eggs when it was complete and replacing it with dummies. The real eggs were brought to point of hatch under a broody bantam where they could be protected and then replaced under the sitting partridge. In this way the clutch was spared the risks of weather and predation during the incubation period. The old way was more labour intensive and involved some serious praying for sunshine in Royal Ascot week which was when most of the eggs hatched. An early June thunderstorm could wipe out most of the chicks.

Back on the rearing field the chicks were hatching. Plaintive piping came from beneath the feathers of the foster mothers and tiny heads peeped out into the strange new world. Labour now was intensified. This was before the days of the concentrated, high protein foods which a keeper can now buy off the shelf. To give the chicks the nourishment they needed Sam spent his days boiling rabbits in a copper and mincing the meat finely. He did the same to eggs, hard-boiling, shelling and chopping them. He gathered ants' eggs and mixed the lot with dry rusk until it was crumbly to the touch. This was fed to the broods and contained all the nourishment they needed.

Every day this task was repeated and the romance of the keeper's life seems far removed from the drudgery of constant food preparation. The hutches had to be moved regularly to fresh grass when the old places became fouled. Watch was kept on the field twenty-four hours a day: no flock of sheep at lambing time

was better protected. The gun was never far from hand and let a sparrowhawk flicker over, tawny owl roost overhead or rat emerge from the bushes attracted by the sight and smell of so much food, and it fell to a well-placed charge of shot. Often in summer Sam was working an eighteen-hour day.

After six weeks the fast growing poults would be taken in crates by pony and trap to the release pens, large wire enclosures dotted about the woodlands, where they could be acclimatised to the wild and become more independent. They needed feeding but now were weaned onto corn and the minced rabbit regime was over. Foxes were kept at bay and the headkeeper mixed with the corn a secret recipe passed down from generations which he was convinced would prevent his birds from straying. This mixture, of which aniseed was the biggest ingredient, was kept in a large bottle which was never let out of his sight.

As the birds trickled out of the release pen, Sam had to go round twice a day with a dog and send them back home, tapping down the hedgerows and ditches down which they wandered. He had been given his first gun, a trusty old hammer weapon belonging to the headkeeper and polished silver with use. After dogging-in he was dispatched to keep the woodpigeons from eating the ripening corn. In this way he became a useful shot; having a natural aptitude and living in the company of other good shots he had every incentive.

Autumn saw the start of shooting season and young Sam in his estate-issue tweeds was the humblest beater, whacking through the woods and over stubbles with his flag, moving the partridges towards the waiting gentry. As years passed he rose through the ranks, acted as loader for one of the Guns and worked his dogs, of which by then he had a quartet of three springers and a Labrador. He sorted out the game at the end of the day, bracing the birds and seeing them safely to the game larder. Eventually he was given responsiblity for his own beat and when Grimes retired he took over as head man.

Winter saw shooting season in full swing with the big pheasant days. This was also the time for night poaching, when ruffians from the mining town came out with their lamps and .410s to shoot the roosting birds from the trees. Sam could remember many a battle in the moonlit woodlands but more often it was a story of frozen vigils on bitter nights when nobody came. The estate earned the reputation of having a team of tough and resourceful keepers. Word spread and the poachers chose less well defended places for their predations. Sam appeared as a witness in court and in later life was made a Special Constable.

Now in his mid-sixties but still not retired, Sam leaned on the gate to the old rearing field and reflected on how his job had changed. The paddock, once so lovingly manicured, was a mass of thorn and rioting weeds which would have made old Grimes turn in his grave. Rearing now was done in an incubator which did all the work and chicks were warmed by gas or electricity. Apart from foxes, which he shot at night with his rifle from the back of his Land Rover, he bothered less with vermin as rearing large numbers of birds was a more effective use of his time. Food was mass-produced high-protein pellets so no more mincing rabbits or hunting for ants' eggs.

Rabbits had been decimated by myxomatosis, the gibbet had long been abandoned as a figment of the worst of the bad old days and even poachers came rarely – the price of game did not merit the risk. A keeper would as soon give you a few brace and save you the trouble of a moonlight foray when you could all be safe in bed. The passing car-window shooter was the worst of his worries on that score.

His lordship's friends who made up the old shooting parties had been replaced by a syndicate. They had the money to keep the shooting going but lacked the skills and sometimes, he thought, the manners of the old-time gentry. He was content enough, for they paid his wages and his lordship still had three days for his old friends which were the ones that Sam enjoyed most. The bags were smaller than of old but he had been instructed to show high birds with none of the flappers which used to feature early in the year. The grey partridges had all but gone due to changes in the way the land was farmed, but he reared redlegs to take their place. More than anything else he missed the little brown birds of his youth.

Sparrowhawks thrived as did owls and many other birds of prey which now were safe from him. Old Grimes would have had a fit. The gin trap had gone to be replaced by the humane Fenn trap, and crows and magpies he caught in the Larsen, which did his nesting songbirds a good turn.

He did not himself shoot much any more, preferring to improve habitats, organise his shooting days and continue a great tradition of countryside stewardship. Without the likes of his estate, as a nation, we might not enjoy the rich diversity of wildlife, from orchids to frogs and marsh harriers to blackcaps which, in season, he could see on his rounds.

His old mates had gone, leaving him to accomplish alone what it had taken a small army of them to do when he was a boy. Sam lived in old Grimes' cottage and felt a sense of continuity in his profession. His only worry was that his son had shown no interest in the old ways but sought employment in industry far from home. His job changed out of recognition in half a century but the basic tenets of good management, to create and maintain a countryside which is the envy of Europe, had remained faithful.

The Hare in the Furrow

The brown hare is a curious fellow. 'A hopper of ditches, a cropper of corn, a little brown cow with a pair of leather horns', runs the old rhyme. From ancient times the hare has been a potent symbol in country lore. 'Puss' as she was known, for all hares irrespective of gender are referred to as female, was bound up with old mythology, witches and the full moon. It was said, for example, that rather than turn into a cat which many held wrongly to be her 'familiar', a witch would become a hare when she wished to travel the parish at night. There was rumour of just such a thing in a village near Cambridge. An ancient crone lived in a cottage at the bottom of a green lane. Like any lonely old woman she mumbled to herself a fair bit and in those superstitious times was said to have the evil powers.

A great and beautiful hare was in the habit of running through the orchard every evening in the direction of her hovel. It was obvious that this was the old woman in her second shape. The locals did their best to ambush this beast but she always got the better of them, leaving the orchard by different routes and evading traps with an uncanny sixth sense, fuelling the theory of supernatural powers.

Some old codger recalled that you needed a silver bullet to kill the 'Evil One' and he loaded his old muzzle loader with two silver buttons taken from his waistcoat. Again the hare came streaking through, this time within range, the shot sped true, the hare rolled over with an unearthly scream, and lay dead. At that selfsame moment the cottage of the old crone burned to the ground and she died with a hideous shriek at the same moment as the hare. What further proof could a man need?

A wounded hare will give fearsome, childlike screams which make the blood run cold, a trait which strengthens its link with humans. For this reason there are many hard-headed sportsmen who will never raise their gun to old puss as she comes streaking out on a partridge drive. She is too noble a creature to be bowled over thoughtlessly, her brown fur or 'fleck' blowing sadly across the stubble and anyway, few today have the stomach for that strong, dark meat.

In his poem, *The Eve of St Agnes*, Keats wrote that 'The hare limped trembling through the frozen grass', but in fact a hare is proof against very bad weather indeed. Like an Eskimo she will make a nest or form in the snow and snuggle down out of the wind, her ears flat conserving warmth and even after the most

bitter winters her numbers seem not to suffer. Apart from man her main enemies are foxes and in the north of Britain, eagles. A fox will work a stubble or hay meadow at night and pick a hare from a form or more often a leveret from where its mother has left it.

The hare has a wonderful and spectacular courtship. Like most wooings it is Nature's way of seeing that only the best males get the chance to pass on the strongest genes, but it is pretty to watch. Many hares will gather in a favoured field, two males will face up to each other and engage in a lightning boxing match, standing on their long hind legs, their forepaws a blur as they spar until the fur flies. They bump into each other, one leaping clear over an opponent as they joust. They rush round in circles chasing each other, first one then another in front, behaving so strangely that long ago someone coined the expression 'as mad as a March hare'. It was no accident that the March hare was one of the guests at the surreal tea party in *Alice in Wonderland*.

The doe deposits her three or four leverets in different places on the not-all-eggs-in-one-basket theory of survival. She stays well away from them by day leaving them to lie as still as stones, their delicate brown fur blending with the dead weeds and bleached grass. Their safety lies in being able to remain motionless even when a predator passes close. One movement would catch the eye of a fox and – no more leveret. If the youngster stays still there is a good chance that it will be overlooked. The mother comes to them in turn at night to suckle them until they begin to eat grass and vegetation and look after themselves. Some damage is done by neo-countryfolk who may live in villages but think Beaconsfield, who happen on a leveret left by its mother and take it home in the belief that it is lost or abandoned. This is one cause of leveret mortality for invariably they die.

This creature of the moon, beloved of old, cold goddesses has other strange habits. It gnaws its own dung, deriving secondary nutrition from partly digested pellets. When coursed it takes not the easy way running downhill but sets off up a steep slope, her powerful back legs proof against all pursuers in a straight race; she is the swiftest mammal in the countryside. Old timers believed she could be male and female at one and the same time and slept with her eyes open. She has a preference always for the same field. Let a hare die on its own ground and there will be another in its place in a week.

They have their favourite places. An old farmer lay dying, his sons clustered round his bedside to hear his last words, some nugget of philosophy gleaned after eighty years in the countryside. His moment came and feebly he beckoned his eldest son near. He bent down to hear the great secret, maybe buried treasure or an unexpected bequest. With his dying breath, in a voice barely audible, the old man whispered, 'Dew yew allus look an oat stubble for a heere…' and with that he passed away. It was the most valuable and certain piece of information he could pass down to the next generation.

The hare has been sporting quarry since before the Pharaohs. William Twyti, huntsman for Uther Pendragon, was said to have preferred the hare to all the great boars, stags and wolves in the forest. He was intrigued by her ways and skill at eluding her enemies.

While the pursuit of hares by a yeoman with a broken-coated lurcher was the old way of getting a dinner, true coursing is done not with the object of catching hares but relishing the skills of the pursuing greyhounds. Should the greyhounds happen to kill the hare it is a matter for regret, for no longer can the hounds show their speed on the turn or fleetness of foot. As for beagling, the hare has time to stop and nibble at the grass during the hunt while far behind a pack of miniature hounds with human foot followers are bogged down in the middle of 50 acres of heavy ploughing as securely as flies on a fly paper. The last hare caught by our local pack was back in the 1950s and that was on its last legs with age and infirmity.

Her real enemy, as of so much wildlife, is modern farming which poisons and rapes the good earth until the very creatures that depend upon it sicken and die. Surprisingly enough the largest populations of the healthiest hares are found on land which is managed for coursing or estates which are strictly keepered.

To the Victorian cottager a hare was less a creature of romance

and more a hearty meal on four legs. When meat was rarely on the table a hare could feed a large family for a week, but the penalties for taking her could be savage. A crafty man would set a snare in the right place in the hedge bottom where puss had her runs. Sometimes he had a long dog which would chase a hare from a field at night and into the net which he had hung from the top rail of the gate.

There were many ways of taking her, from setting a gin trap near a few turnips scattered on a field, to murdering her with a stick as she sat in the form. Serious poachers knew that she loved parsley above anything else. They would scatter seed on an old stubble or a spring corn drill. The plants would be overlooked by the farmer but discovered by every hare in the parish, so the poacher knew every time where to go to find one at night.

'Old Sarah', as she is sometimes called, is still with us and is one of the most conspicuous wild animals we have. Here and there she falls on hard times and there are seasonal fluctuations of numbers – nobody quite knows why. The great hare shoots of twenty years ago when they were slain by the many hundreds in a day on account of crop damage have largely become things of the past.

Good to eat, a sporting beast without equal, full of curiosities and old myths, the brown hare has in her a scrap of ancient magic which in a hard-headed, commercial age we ought to treasure.

The Old School

It stood at the bottom of School Lane, a red and yellowish brick building with a curious tiled spire halfway along, making it look like a whim of an architect used to designing Methodist chapels. That spire served no purpose other than ornament and to house the school bell, the long rope of which hung down into the classroom neatly made off on a cleat on the wall. For a pupil to lay so much as a finger on it brought dire penalties. Outside was the regulation rectangle of asphalt, then the coke shed and along one side a line of outside privies.

Each morning little figures emerged from cottages along the High Street and from down the lanes which led off it and set off singly, met up with others, became a trickle then a tide all flooding in the same direction. With ten minutes to go the bell tolled a dozen strokes. After five more minutes it rang again, so you knew you had to hurry.

That walk to school, which took some of us a quarter of an hour, was itself what today they call a 'learning experience', one denied most modern youngsters. Parents are concerned about the dangers of modern living, the fear of abduction and of being run over, sad testaments to our civilised world. The pupils now are taken to school by car, those living nearby led by a protective hand not to be released until the school gate. At the end of the afternoon they are collected in the same way.

Then the walk to school was an adventure. Time passed in animated conversation and a reliving of last night's episode of *Dick Barton, Special Agent*, the quarter of an hour early evening slot later occupied by *The Archers*. You played games, set ambushes and dropped from overhanging boughs onto the next scholar hurrying along. In autumn it was a chance for conker competitions of Homeric proportions while a bird's nest high in a tree could not be passed without investigation. We had to cross the stream by the footbridge, an opportunity for some desultory paddling or adding a new section to the dam we were building.

There were elder sticks to be cut and used for sword fights until the soft wood splintered and flew into shreds all over the path. Bows and arrows were made and used to dangerous effect. The best arrows had weight in the tips to make them stick in the ground. Ideal for this were scraps of lead from the stained glass window in the east end of the church which had blown out when a bomber exploded in the war. The fragments lay in the grass among the gravestones and as the parson's son I had a monopoly.

So engrossed could we become that the second bell might find us in the middle of a pitched battle, a dozen a side. Weapons were cast down and we dashed the quarter of a mile to school to

tumble into the classroom rosy-cheeked and panting, with muddy knees and shining eyes. It was a good start to the day, one denied children in these sanitised days.

Miss Vye taught the titches. She seemed a very old lady but when you are five years old every adult seems aged. She wore a long black dress, her hair in a severe bun, and favoured steel-rimmed spectacles. She was very kind but firm. Six year olds learned the difference between 'there' and 'their' – a simple enough distinction one might think but one which escapes many older and more expensively educated children today.

Then it was on to Mr Spate's class, that silvery-haired, dapper man who wore spats. He was strong on Religious Knowledge and had the ability to enthral his listeners with the tales of David slaying Goliath, Samson pushing down the temple and the desert-hardened Israelites whooping and screaming though the dust, hungry to sack Jericho as the walls came crashing down. There was not much in the lessons about Christianity but they were rattling good yarns all the same.

The heating in the schoolroom was from a pot-bellied, tortoise stove fed by coke from a hod which stood at its side. It had a metal railing round it to prevent careless pupils falling against it. Mr Spate occupied a position with his back to its cosy warmth, while those of us on the back settles shivered, hands clenched in pockets, knobbly knees blue and chapped.

Punishment was meted out by Mr Spate's small but whippy stick which he laid on not for bad behaviour, for it went without saying that in the classroom at least we were good, but for bad work. Failure to complete the right number of sums, of adding up pounds, shillings and pence, was recognised by the public humiliation of being hauled out in front, ordered to touch your toes and being dealt a quick whack on the bottom. The girls watched smugly, knowing that whatever they did they were immune from such treatment.

Free handouts were non-existent but one day in 1945 we were all assembled and each handed a parchment from King George VI himself which opened with the words, 'Today as we celebrate victory…' I had lost mine within the week but I wish I had it now,

especially as this year we are to celebrate the fiftieth anniversary of that great day.

Art was primitive daubing with poster paint on sugar paper; there was no woodwork or even organised games so music was a rare chance to express ourselves. Mrs Smith taught music, another formidable lady dressed all in black with ferocious spectacles. Music was community singing – Mrs Smith on the piano and everyone else belting out the old favourites such as 'The Vicar of Bray', 'Barbara Allen' and a special favourite, 'The Fox and the Goose'. This contained some amusing *double entendres* in the lyrics such as 'Old Mother Knicker-Knacker jumped out of bed, and out of the window she popped her head. . .' At the word 'knicker' we sang especially loudly, barely concealing our sniggers at this freedom in public to use a rude word.

Mrs Smith was alert to such wickedness and had the rare musical ability to leave the piano in mid-tune, fly across the room, administer a stinging slap on the bare thigh of a transgressor and nip back in time for the chorus – without losing a bar. To this day I recall the words of some of those old songs and as I rehearse them in my head I feel a faint tingling on my thigh.

Mr Spate's biblical battles were re-enacted later in the playground doubling with marbles as trials of skill and strength. In winter we made a long ice slide the length of the playground and when an adult slipped over, giving innocent merriment to all, 'the man' came out and put salt on it and spoiled it. One rule which was not to be broken on pain of dire punishment was to throw coke. It lay in a tempting heap in the corner of the playground and while most other missiles were acceptable, coke was not. A fragment might lodge in someone's eye. The ultimate sanction was to be sent to the headmaster, Mr Henry Scott, he who read the lessons in church with the passion and stentorian fervour of an Old Testament prophet.

'Scotty' was always a distant figure, one used to frighten the children and while I left before I aspired to his top class, I am sure he was an old dear with no harm in him. As any school teacher would know, a stern exterior and reputation for unbridled savagery so that your name is spoken in whispers is as good a defence as any, although inside you might be as gentle as a suckling lamb.

I left after two years, my parents deciding to send me to a posh preparatory school in Cambridge where I boarded. I hated leaving my woods and fields, the conkers, tiddler catching and frog spawn collecting while even 'The Fox and the Goose' suddenly achieved an almost mystical nostalgia. My life now became more patrician in taste and I began to 'talk proper', although I never forgot those good old boys, my mates, with their marbles and their big, iron-shod boots, and I shed a tear for my secret, unrequited loves in their brown sandals, white ankle socks, red ribbons and gingham frocks by the coke sheds.

The Vicarage Garden

Neglected, overgrown and decaying are words which an insensitive visitor might use and the vicar would have resented all of them. He would remind you of the old days when the vicar was a man of substance, and his twenty-eight-roomed vicarage was built and gardens laid out when staff to do the work could be hired for a few shillings a week. The gardens alone were kept in order by three men and a boy. He did his best single-handed by becoming an almost full-time gardener himself, but so much as hint at the word 'neglected', and this mild-mannered man might have bridled.

Outside the tall windows of the dining hall and drawing room are terraced lawns. Two mown banks run down to a wide expanse of grass. Beyond it is a bosky spinney where the nightingale sings in summer and where the great elms and lime trees housing the rookery stand, purple-budded in spring, green-canopied and abuzz with bees in high summer. On each far corner of the lawn rears a giant wellingtonia, the two tallest trees in the village. Their dry pulpy bark, which you can rip off in flakes, is ideal nesting for spotted flycatchers which made summer afternoons a joy as they hawk insects, using the top of a cricket stump for a launch post.

Behind one of these trees stands the old summer house, now fallen in and dilapidated. Its wooden floor and roominess suggest Edwardian tea parties when the wellingtonia, which now towers above it, was but a few feet tall. Beyond the rookery spinney is the churchyard with the sexton's log cabin where he kept the tools of his grim trade, and round it the ranks of gravestones where the ancients of the village take their final rest from their labours.

Turn left at the house and walk along a wide gravelled path, down two sets of stone steps, down the slope past an ancient mulberry, a magnificent Scots pine and a solitary beech and you come to the tennis court. You could tell where it was by the rectangular enclosure with metal posts leaning rakishly and the remains of brown and rusty wire tangled in the grass. The lawn once mown smooth, echoed to happy cries and the thwack of racquets as ladies in long dresses and picture-hats scooped the ball back and forth. Now it has gone to seed, covered in tussocks so luxuriant that a partridge nested there and brought off a lusty brood of chicks. The posts which supported the net stand there still, leaning drunkenly at an angle, never to be used again.

Look right and you see a long greenhouse like a wrecked ocean liner with much of the glass broken and the once snowy woodwork green and black with age. At one end is a flag pole with a knob on top. Large enough to make a horticulturist a living today, it was once used purely for domestic purposes.

Go inside, if you dare risk a shard of glass falling on your head, and wonder at the row of iron pipes through which flowed the hot water that kept it warm in winter. By the door, stone steps lead down to the boiler room where an iron fire box which would have served *The Lusitania* stands quietly rusting. The tables and racks which were once a forest of blooms and cuttings now have but a tray of the vicar's seed potatoes, a handful of geraniums in pots and some brassica plants ready for pricking out.

Beyond the greenhouse lies a cobbled yard. Once it boasted a cottage where the coachman lived. In his kitchen hung a brass bell which the vicar could ring by pulling a rope in his study to let the coachman know that he wished his conveyance to be made ready. In my youth there was a dog cart in the shed, in sound order generally but one shaft was broken and the leather cushions covered in green mould with tufts of horsehair sticking through the rents nibbled by mice. At the far end of the yard are three large coach houses. The vehicles have long gone and one building is full of chickens, the other wood and the third a garage for the family Morris eight. Not many houses in the village could be said to keep their car, logs and hens in buildings more than good enough for human habitation. A pair of tall double gates leads out onto the lane but they have sagged on their hinges and are kept permanently open. Grass grows in tufts between the cobbles and the mellowing red brick of the walls is quietly flaking away.

Return through the green door, back past the greenhouse and turn right again. Follow the yew hedge which becomes box, past another stand of tall trees and you come to the kitchen garden. In its day this would provide more than enough vegetables for a large household. There is an old but still productive asparagus bed, a run of cold-frames and the red, rusty remains of an iron trellis where rambling roses grew. The gardeners are long gone and the vicar himself with the reluctant aid of his son dig as much as they can each autumn. It is heavy, clay land and one spadeful is enough to make you grunt. By a superhuman effort rows of potatoes, greens, carrots, peas and beans appear each summer. The rabbits are kept off the more sensitive plants by wire defences which would not have looked out of place on the Somme.

Beyond the vegetable garden is another dense swathe of woodland with an overgrown pond and a wealth of fine old trees, for one vicar a century ago had been an avid planter of exotic species. There is an ancient medlar – so easy to climb – and a fine walnut, yews, spindle, thorn and the universal elm suckers, the forest floor covered with a carpet of dark green ivy. In spring aconites and snowdrops speckle the ground with gold and white.

A hedge and path mark the boundary of the kitchen garden and beyond it lies a 2 acre meadow rented by a local farmer Mr Randall for his cows. In the corner is a horse pond with a great willow standing by it and another fallen to lie across it like a bridge. This is a good place for catching newts and gathering frog spawn and every year a moorhen nests in the young rushes on the margin. Mr Randall did not care for people to wander in his field, so expeditions had to be made by stealth and a hasty retreat beaten should his burly figure appear on the horizon shouting dire threats.

31

Beyond the field and the woodland lies the road. Stroll back along the garden path and you come across a clutch of pigsties, roofed with pantiles, each luxuriously appointed. There were usually two pigs in residence, for in those days many folk kept a pig to eat the scraps and keep them in fat bacon during the winter. In the loft above the sties is a colony of doves, once domesticated homing pigeons but now feral and self-sufficent: there are holes in the brickwork by which they come and go. If anyone appears unexpectedly round the corner staggering with a bucket of pig swill they go clattering off the eaves like a shower of brown, black and white pebbles shot from a gun.

The lime between the bricks in the cavity wall is missing at one point, a hole big enough for a finger to be squeezed in, and a colony of bees has taken up residence. We tried to get them out but with no success. They were safe in their stone fortress.

Later, after a storm damaged the wall, a whole brick fell out and a stock dove took to nesting there.

In the black winter of 1947 we had knee-deep snow and a hurricane screamed over the whole of East Anglia leaving serious flooding in its wake. Both the giant wellingtonias which had sighed and whispered in many a summer sun came crashing down. As these giants lay toppled, their topmost fronds brushed the dining room windows. Some great elms succumbed and the last few bits of glass fell from the greenhouse roof or went skittering across the road, a fearful risk to passers-by.

The old vicarage garden is a magic place for birds for they like those sorts of places. Warblers nest in the rough grass, blackcaps and chiffchaffs sing in spring. There are flycatchers, cuckoos, robins, wrens, tits which nest every year in the hollow mulberry, woodpigeons, stockdoves, rooks, jackdaws in the chimneys, a sparrowhawk, barn and tawny owls, mallard, martins under the eaves, swallows in the sheds, moorhens and every common lowland bird on the British list. For a birdwatcher it is heaven and the vicar's son has the best collection of birds' eggs in the village.

To maintain this gently decaying wilderness is hard labour. The lawn is kept short with a tired old Atco and the formal flower beds with their Queen Alexandra roses were lovingly cared for. The kitchen garden is beaten into some sort of submission and weeds pulled from the gravel closest to the house. The rest is left to itself.

A real effort is made every July before the church garden fête. On that day the lawn was gay with the striped awnings of stalls, the brass band played under the elms, clock golfers negotiated the bumps, the maypole stood proud and hundreds of village folk tramped about on the grass, nervously eyeing the heavens for signs of rain. Even the old greenhouse was pressed into service. You were charged 3d at the door to 'Come and see the water otter'. The curious and gullible paid and went in and there was a tank of water full of weeds. From it trailed a length of rope. The cash customer pulled on this and out came a rusty old kettle full of holes. There, sure enough, was your 'water 'otter'.

That vicar was my father, that old vicarage my home and the rambling garden my playground for the first twenty years of my life. It was paradise for a youngster with an interest in birds and owner of a BSA Cadet air rifle. You had only to walk a few paces from the back door and the jungle would swallow you up and new adventures begin. Tree houses and camps were built, bows and arrows made and Robin Hood battles waged with other boys: trees were climbed and ponds dredged. The lawn was the scene of Homeric cricket matches but you were out if you hit the ball into the nettles. I would come in at tea time with bloodied knees, nettle bumps, rent shorts and hair like a shock of wheat but with rosy cheeks and shining eyes.

It is sad that children today do not have such opportunities but their lives seem ruled by computer games and the TV screen. They were the good old days all right but the trouble was that we did not know it at the time. Then it seemed as though it would always be there and life like that would go on for ever. The lesson is that the good old days are now, so make the most of them.

As for that railway station of a vicarage with its twenty-eight rooms, attics, cellars and range of outhouses along with the 4 acres of garden which was my world, it was all sold. A builder threw up twenty-eight houses on the site and the woods, ponds, newts, birds, mulberry and walnut, the pigsties, greenhouse and cobbled coach-yard are gone as though they had never existed.

Frog Hall Marsh

It is good to see the frogs and toads hopping back into our lives. It is thanks to modern farming that they fell on hard times, but sometimes, almost by accident some struggling creature is given a hand up. The nightjar or goatsucker, that scarce and curious nocturnal bird, has been enjoying a run of record breeding seasons since the great October gales of 1987. The tangle of fallen timber was just the habitat it needed. Similarly the brown hare recovered when the controversial set-aside came into being; the fallow land was just right for them. Creatures which are finding life difficult may be given a reprieve by an accident of fate. The frog was saved by the garden pond.

In the 1960s frogs and toads became scarce. The reasons were the draining of wetlands and the run-off of agricultural chemicals which poisoned the watercourses and killed off the insects on which they depended. To see a frog became a cause for comment and a letter to the local paper. Fifty years ago it was very different. The quiet marshes were a threnody of croaking on mild spring nights and many a marshman fell asleep to that not unpleasant lullaby. As for their spawn, they squirted it indiscriminately in any patch of water upon which they happened, from horse ponds to flooded cart tracks in muddy gateways.

Every junior school in the land had its resident jamjar of the stuff so that the children could see daily the development of the egg through its various stages until it became a fully fledged tadpole. Then came the loss of tail, development of legs and change of shape and there you had your miniature frog which was returned to the wild. Many of them did not achieve this status and died for a variety of reasons but thousands of youngsters learned more firsthand about metamorphosis by seeing the real thing than they would have done from a shelf full of arid text books.

As science students many were to encounter the frog again. It was the favourite subject for biology classes, easy to dissect, with clearly defined central nervous system and muscle structure which made it ideal for the laboratory. Both the keeping of tadpoles and frog dissection have become passé and are outlawed due to an excess of conservationist zeal and the power of the animal rights movement. While one might agree that frogs have certain rights, it is equally true that a valuable teaching aid has been taken from us.

The old pike anglers had a trick which was harder to defend. They would stitch a frog to their hook using fine thread so that the

creature was not damaged. Cast out gently and persuaded to swim about in a jerky fashion it could be a deadly lure for a pike resistant to all other baits. This method too has been abandoned as unnecessarily cruel and few would argue with that.

The frog is the universal fall guy, for everything likes to eat it. The reason it produces a huge amount of spawn is that there is such a low survival rate. If one egg from a hundred matures into a fully grown frog, that is about the best you can expect. The rest are eaten by other creatures which need to fatten up after a hard winter and get into shape for breeding. Grass snakes, herons, fish, eels, rats, weasels, stoats, dragonfly larvae and even owls and foxes will eat frogs or their spawn. Nature provides this bounty for all these creatures, taking the gamble that enough tadpoles will survive to ensure the future of the species.

Like many of the oppressed of the world the frog is a survivor and it came through the hard times and is returning to strength. One reason is that farm sprays are more closely controlled. The deadly insecticides of the 1960s have been outlawed and many things have benefited. The other factor has been the rash of suburban garden ponds. These are ideal for frogs being predator free, apart from the odd goldfish and visiting heron, and they are safe from chemical sprays. Every pond down my road has been full of spawn these last few years, some of them solid globules of the stuff.

My wild marsh pond on a little piece of heaven I call Hunter's Fen ought to be an ideal place for them and I begged buckets of spawn and seeded the shallows. I did this for three years, for frogs have a three-year breeding cycle and I wanted continuity. Sure enough the pond became alive with frogs which croaked away in the evenings, squatted clamped together in passionate embrace in spring, and laid spawn round the weedy margins. I had also introduced some common and mirror carp. Quite small at first, they waxed mightily until some of them grew to over twenty pounds in weight. To such monsters frog spawn was irresistible and they sucked it in through their great soft mouths until the frogs faded to one or two hardy survivors and I found no more spawn.

Not to be beaten, I dug another pond of about half an acre, separated from the original one by an earth dam. The new pond was to be kept fish-free and be a nursery for invertebrates. This is the first year of the experiment and I have been tapping on doors with my plastic bucket and have taken ten large consignments down to my pond and poured them in. The spawn needs to be in the shallows; in deep water it is likely to sink to colder levels where it is less likely to hatch. No doubt the resident moorhen and mallard will take a few but the majority have, as we say in the country, 'two chances'.

A neighbour with a small pond gave me a dollop of toad spawn. This differs from frog spawn in that it is laid in long strings and wound round the water plants. There is no way you can extricate it so you need to snip off the plant at its root, take the lot and mingle it with existing growth in the new place. Toads have their favourite breeding ponds and they think nothing of braving the horrors of a main road to return to it year after year, suffering much slaughter in the process. Conservationists mount guard and convey them across in buckets, holding up the traffic like lollipop ladies. They erect notices by the roadside warning motorists. A lumbering toad is no match for a speeding Ford Escort and as a breeding proposition your chances are significantly reduced once you have become embossed into the tarmac.

It would be good to think that as well as a flourishing froggery my new pond might become a toad breeding site. As there is no road bigger than a cart track nearby they have nothing to fear from the motorist. In time some of the more attractive predators might follow, such as grass snakes, another creature which has suffered due to modern farming. It is good to sit by an old pond on a mild evening in late March and listen to the frogs' chorus and share a simple pleasure known to our ancestors. Who knows, these frogs may be descendants of the same ones that serenaded the spring before the Dutchmen came to drain the fens.

Once I had a Labrador which was fascinated by frogs. Let me overturn an old log and disturb one and Drake's ears cocked and his eyes started as though about to fall from his head. He tapped the frog gently with his paw and when it hopped on he would stalk it. Sometimes he would take it gently in his mouth and bring it to me and he never tired of the game.

He was cured when he tried the same trick with a toad. A toad is not such a push-over as a frog and does not care to be seized, even in such a black velvet bag which did duty as Drake's mouth. The toad went into its defence routine, emitting a fearful frothy substance from its skin which seemed to react with the dog's saliva. Hastily the toad was spat out and the dog rushed about madly, forcing his face through the grass to remove the noxious stuff from his lips. Drake tried it only twice with toads after which he left both frogs and toads well alone.

Spring would not be spring for a countryman until he has heard that mellow, homely croaking and found the first globule of polka-dotted jelly, a symbol of rebirth, lying among the lily pads.

Messengers

For as long as he could remember Albert had farmed his few sandy, windswept acres of Norfolk, competing with the rabbits for his sparse crops, a countryman to his bones, wise in the ways of the world of Nature. His seasons were marked not only by changing weather, the ritual of the farming calendar and the blooming then fading of the hedgerow blossoms but by the movements of the birds. Their arrivals and departures meant much to him. Scraps of feathered magic suddenly in a previously untenanted sky were talismans which spoke to him of change more strongly than any mark in his diary.

One September he had been fishing on a Scottish lowland loch noted for its brown trout and had been privileged to see what few locals had witnessed, the arrival of the pink-footed geese. The great birds nested far north on the central plains of Iceland, migrating south to Britain in autumn when the snows returned and the brief Arctic summer was over.

They are birds of great romance and beauty with huge pinions and strong sinews meant for battling across oceans. They defy our bitterest winters, roosting out in the howling darkness of lonely estuaries, beating in from the tide in great skeins, calling wildly with a sound to stir the soul of the most insensitive listener. Partly for their magic, grey geese are much pursued by wildfowlers for they are wary, cunning and hard to shoot as well as good to eat. The young birds are best in the kitchen, for an old-timer might be a score of years old and as tough as a leather boot.

Albert sat in a boat bobbing on the ripples, when within a few minutes the weather changed. It was mid-afternoon but the sky went as black as night; cars on the main road put on their headlights for some cataclysmic storm was coming. Albert looked round for his coat. There was one gap in the black canopy, straight overhead, a hand's breadth of blue sky fringed with black and mauve where lightning flickered. Suddenly, far off he heard the familiar, double cry, that sharp yelp which made his scalp prickle and so stirs the blood of fowlers.

Staring up he saw a tiny speck in the sky, whiffling and spiralling down through that single gap in the clouds. Behind it was another and another and then a great company of them, all swinging round, losing height and tumbling down with joyful bugling towards the water. Almost down, they banked into the wind, settled on the surface and drank heavily for they were dehydrated after their saga. Then each put its grey head under its wing and fell asleep. In ten minutes the loch which had held only a handful of resident coots was dotted with a thousand pink-footed geese all asleep, some close to his boat for they had no fear of man, the birds hatched that year never before having seen a human being. By the end of the week there were ten thousand of them flying out to feed at dawn and back to the safety of the loch at dusk.

Albert knew now that winter was coming for although the trees were heavy in leaf and the hedges peppered with hips and haws, the summer was dying and the arrival of the grey geese was the first clear message that the cold, fog, ice and snow would be here sooner rather than later.

The winter came and went, Easter was almost here and he was leaning on the gate gazing at his herd of slab-sided bullocks when something made him look up. There in the grey sky was a tiny chip of black, a splinter of coal zipping across the sky, swooping round and down and back over the meadow. It was the first swallow of summer and while he knew that the hot weather was still a few weeks away he saw in this little bird the ancient promise fulfilled that the year was rolling round. It spoke to him of long evenings,

41

of deckchairs, the click of bat on ball on the village green, of strawberries and the scent of freshly cut hay.

He was sure that this was one of the pair which nested every year in his old barn. It was one of the miracles of Nature, even now not fully explained, how a tiny bird with a brain weighing a fraction of an ounce could find its way from South Africa where it wintered, back not only to his own country but to the county, village, lane and the same beam in the very barn it had occupied last year. Challenge Albert to walk from his barn to South Africa and he would have wandered off course before he reached Dover.

Long ago, country folk were at a loss to explain the mysteries of bird migration. They could not comprehend the miracle that a bird could accomplish a feat they could never do. They decided that swallows and martins swooped down into the ponds, lakes and rivers, diving down and sinking into the mud where they remained comatose until the coming of spring. The fact that swallows often skimmed the water, taking insects off the surface, seeming to kiss their own reflections, was further proof that they were preparing for the time when they sank beneath the ripples for the winter.

By Albert's time the secret was common knowledge but that great trek grew more arduous every year. The Sahara desert expanded, the casualty rate of the migrants grew and fewer seemed to make it back in spring to the old ledges and rafters in barns and cart sheds up and down the land. Albert wondered whether by the time his granddaughter was as old as he, the barn swallow would come no more. He knew that there were at least a dozen members of the swallow family all but three of which had no urge to migrate but spent the whole year in Africa. Summer in England would not be the same without that first messenger, that tiny spirit of the wheeling year.

The cuckoo was another potent symbol of spring. The crazy calling of the old 'gowk' from whose name the word cuckold is derived, meant that privation and hard times were over. He came when summer was trembling on the brink of bursting out and the buds were opening. Some old timers in a West Country hamlet decided that if they could but capture the cuckoo who brought with him the good weather, they would enjoy summer all year round. Accordingly they built a fence around him as he sat on a bush. The fence was all but done when the bird rose and with a flick of his wings skimmed out over the top and away. The village ancient shook his head wisely. 'I told you that fence were too low. Another foot higher and you'd a' got 'im.'

House martins arrived a week or two before the first swallow. There were precious few insects for them to eat in mid-March and they received a cold welcome after their long journey. One morning Albert would wake and hear the familiar twittering as the first pair investigated the remains of their old nest over his bedroom window. Two black and white bottoms in their smart waiters' suits pressed against the pane.

Often they built above a window rather than on the plain wall next to it and over the summer their droppings and those of their numerous broods accumulated, becoming a thick scarf of chalky black and white on the window frame. Folk in the posh new houses on the estate would hang polythene bags from their upstairs windows as frighteners to keep the birds away. 'The mess rots your paintwork, you know', they would cry from the tops of ladders. Not so Albert who felt it a privilege to be their host for a few short months.

One morning he woke to find that all was not well with his domestic idyll. The contented chittering had an anxious note and there was the voice of a stranger, strident and aggressive. Slowly he drew back the curtain to find his pair of martins hovering and flickering round the entrance of their mud nest, crying their agitation. From the portal protruded the head of a house sparrow, cursing them roundly. Sparrows are noted thieves of martin nests and will occupy any likely hole which saves them the trouble of making a home for themselves. By nature they are as aggressive as martins are mild-mannered and the victims have no chance of ejecting the squatters by confrontation.

Albert had read of a pair of martins which had in their veins the blood of heroes. When their nest was taken over by sparrows they fetched mud from the field gateway and bit by bit walled up the sitting hen while she sat. In time the entrance was closed and the interloper walled in, facing certain death as a punishment for house stealing. Albert's martins were not made of such iron stuff being meek and unheroic with no weapon save a pathetic twittering and hovering round their home.

Pesky sparrows he had a-plenty; martins were few and to be cherished. Albert thought long and hard and next morning saw him lurking in his front porch armed with his old Daisy air rifle. He could see the nest through the slats up which grew the rambling rose. He did not wish his shot to damage the nest although the owners would have made all snug again: he wanted it to be a clean job.

After ten minutes one sparrow poked out her head to shout defiance at the martins. The rifle popped and the squatter came fluttering down to fall in the herbaceous border. He reloaded and waited, for longer this time but then the cock bird came and sat on the guttering, peering down to see where 'herself' had got to. Again the rifle spoke, the crumb of lead sped true, there was a little thud and a puff of pale feathers and sparrow number two fell back to lie on the tiles. For all Albert knows or cares he lies there still.

The martins returned, peace reigned once more, the meek had inherited the earth. Had Albert interfered with the balance of Nature? He admitted that it might have been so, but to protect his little birds, those who had travelled thousands of miles just to honour him by nesting under his roof, he would have done much. Along with the cuckoo, who would soon be here to shout his lunatic call from the willows, the wild geese, the swallows, warblers and turtle doves spoke to him of new seasons, of the rolling round of the country year and reminded him of tasks he had to do and preparations to make.

His swallows were safe in his barn, the martins snug beneath his eaves. Albert heaved a sigh of relief. At least now he knew that the arrival of at least this summer was guaranteed.

Summer

With the trees heavy in leaf and cottage gardens blazing with the glory of summer flowers, it is hard to recall the bleak bareness of winter. Days are long, evenings sultry and the fly fisherman is on the river bank in the gloaming tempting a trout, its caution momentarily dulled by the flood of insects.

The old village folk tend their peas and beans and keep the hoe busy. Those with surplus which cannot be stored send punnets of soft fruit and bundles of runner beans to market on the Puffing Billy which chugs daily through the village. The bee keeper attends to his little kingdom, meting out justice to his subjects and seeing to their needs, the most benign of dictators. The carp in the lake are busy, for they too are creatures of the summer. Carp anglers, their minds vacant of all thoughts but those of bronzed giants of the green depths, sit hunched and graven beneath umbrellas.

Roads are dusty, and the distant murmur of children's voices from the dame school is as soothing as any lullaby; and tilting a battered straw hat over his eyes, a man at ease with himself and the world lies back in a deck chair beneath the apple tree, and closes his eyes.

The Fenland Flyer

It was Dr Beeching who put an end to it all. The country used to be seamed with little railway lines connecting sleepy wayside halts one to another, providing rural transport which preceded the buses, was reliable and cheap to use. No doubt the good doctor was right and they were wildly uneconomic but with their passing our village was one of many which lost something it valued.

We called her the Fenland Flyer, the little train which puffed its way through a string of fen villages stopping at the market towns, ending up in Cambridge or sometimes going on to the Norfolk coast for holiday excursions. On a busy day she came through my village as often as twice. We had a proper railway station with platform and all, an office marked 'Station Master', a garden of blazing summer flowers, frilly wooden canopy overhead and our village name blazoned on a white board, as if anyone did not know where they were.

It stood at the end of the village down Station Road – where else? – and you could stand on the platform and gaze out over the weedy fields where a frieze of brown rush, old potato haulms and wheat stubbles ran to the flat horizon until land and sky seemed to merge. In summer that train bore the heavy responsibility of taking our produce to market. Many folk with cottage gardens or an acre of land worked hard to make a few pounds from their labour. The train would stand hissing to itself in the station while on the platform stood a cornucopia of punnets of strawberries, bundles of chrysanths, baskets of runner beans and trays of eggs.

The door of the single waggon was slid back with much clanking of bolts and our few bits of produce safely stowed inside. By the time it reached the market town it was full of flowers and vegetables, each offering identified with a label showing the owner's name and address. Within a week a cheque for often no more than a few shillings came through the post. In those thrifty days every little helped with straitened family budgets. Now and then you could make a killing if you had something which was in short supply. If your beans were a week early, if you happened on a good stand of field mushrooms or a batch of early goose eggs, prices doubled, but it did not last long. Soon everyone else was in full production.

There were quiet times when there might be only a couple of baskets to collect, together with the usual four milk churns which stood on the platform like dumpy silver policemen. The driver would not go to the trouble of unlocking and heaving back the heavy doors of the waggon; instead he stood the churns on his footplate and took the few baskets of produce into the cab with him. The fireman stoked the boiler, black smoke billowed, the Flyer gave a peremptory whistle and chugged on to the next village and more churns and baskets. By the time it reached the town the engine resembled a travelling harvest festival.

Mr Arnold was station master, gardener and God of that little outpost. He wore the black trousers and waistcoat with heavy silver watch chain of his calling, his ensemble topped by a peaked cap which was the envy of every small boy in the village. He was also verger and head sidesman of the church. He tended the station garden and dealt faithfully and with some importance with his one train a day. He would haul out his watch and stare at the dial as though a few minutes early or late could matter in those lazy days when there always seemed time for everything and we lived not by the clock but by the slow rhythm of the seasons.

His train duly checked, he would knock off early in the afternoon

and with quiet dignity pedal his sit-up-and-beg bicycle to his house in the village. Where most folk had a wicker basket strapped to the handlebars Mr Arnold had a wooden box. In this he would bring home daily a few knobs of coal from the heap in the station yard. It was one of the perks of the job and his roaring open fire was the envy of Pound Lane where he lived.

There was one special day in the year, the combined Sunday School outing and village trip to the seaside. For this the Flyer drew in towing three whole carriages. To go on the outing to Hunstanton on the Norfolk Coast was a reward for children who had gained enough attendance marks in their devotions to qualify. It was a high price to pay every Sunday when we could have been out bird-nesting or ferreting but as the day of the outing drew near suddenly it seemed worthwhile.

An excited throng gathered on the station; Mr Arnold had donned his black jacket for the occasion. He frowned at his watch, there came a distant whistle and the Flyer came chugging round the bend and pulled into the station with a burst of steam and a clanking of metal. Then came the rush for seats for we all wanted to be not only next to a friend but next to a window. All in, a head count made and we were off. The long wait and then a burst of smoke, a toot, and the station began to move slowly past, gathering speed until it slid away behind and green and brown fields took its place.

Some clutched buckets and spades, mothers stowed great picnic baskets, the men were in their best suits, for this was before the days of open necked shirts and surfing shorts on days out. The flat fens gave way to the sand and pine trees of Norfolk and just when the novelty of the journey was wearing thin we were there, shepherded together on Hunstanton station and ushered down to the beach.

The children dug and paddled, old folk sat in deck chairs, hungry gulls wheeled overhead, ice creams were bought, slot machines played and a crab in a paper bag bought to take home for later. The return journey was of different mood. The excitement of the outward trip gave way to tetchy weariness. My father would organise community singing and in piping trebles we struck up

with 'One man and his dog went to mow a meadow…' until having reached armies of men with packs of dogs going on the same expedition we lost heart. Even 'I Spy' lost its savour while 'Old Macdonald had a Farm' as a musical proposition had been wrung dry. In desperation father tried a 'Keeping Quiet' competition.

Home at last we could see the lights of the village twinkling up on the hill while the great bulk of our Norman church reared against the stars. The train squealed to a halt and wearily, our shoes full of sand, carrying the limp remains of picnics, we tramped up Station Road, youngsters in arms fast asleep, buckets clutched safe but spades all broken at the collar where they had an inherent weakness, until one by one we found our own front gates. The outing was over for another year. It would mean many more hours at Sunday School before the next one.

The railway line had other possibilities. Where it snaked through the lonely fen the fireweed or rose-bay willow-herb flourished, encouraged by bank fires from burning cinders. This was good for pheasants and often we would walk the line as far as we wished, an old Labrador hunting out the banks and many a bird we bagged. Partridges liked to bathe on the dusty gravel between the tracks. When the Flyer approached we stepped to one side until it had passed and driver and fireman gave us a wave and sometimes even stopped for a chat, throwing Mr Arnold's schedules into turmoil. Rabbits too loved railway lines and they burrowed deep beneath the banks. It was a good place to work a ferret for the digging was easy and the rabbits legion.

Then the axe fell, the line closed and the Flyer came no more. The bank remained for years after until bit by bit the farmers took in their own sections and returned them to fields. The metal lines were taken up by the railway people for they were valuable. The abandoned station burned down one day and I could see the plume of smoke from our kitchen window. By this time many people had cars; we had become mobile, so a trip to Hunstanton was no longer the high spot of the year for folk could go almost at will. Cottage-garden produce went on the bus to Ely before that trade too died out, swamped by the mass production of the commercial growers. The market had no interest in your one basket of runner beans or two couple of rabbits.

Mr Arnold and his silver watch were needed no more; the station site was turned into an industrial park with modern buildings. The last of the embankments which carried the track were removed and the Fenland Flyer had gone as though it had never been. It is still possible to walk down Station Road on a hot evening in August and hear in your mind's ear the distant toot as the old girl came panting up the gradient and if you listen very carefully you might just catch the song sung by youngsters who are now themselves grandparents, a ghostly echo of 'One man and his dog…'

Mayfly Time

There is an unspoken, comforting thought which sustains the fly-fisher through hard times. He may shiver in the bitter winds of spring, suffer torrential downpours, August droughts when no fish takes and all the uncertainties of 'back end' fishing but he is quietly confident that when it comes, mayfly time will pay for all.

A mayfly takes two years to mature, two whole years spent as a hideous grub, a predator which slaughters water fleas, the larvae of less aggressive insects and even tadpoles. It is a monster of the stream bed, a bulging-eyed horror with powerful jaws and no mercy. Time passes slowly in its grey, underwater world. Overhead the ice thickens and then thaws, floods roar past, grey dawns and dusks mark the passing of winter days when wind and snow whistle across the dreary fields. Cattle come down to drink in summer and in autumn dead leaves float past in rafts. The mayfly larvae creep in their muddy world, ignorant of life in the open air, preparing for their hour of magic.

Then, one day in late May or early June comes the time, the moment for which the vigil was a preparation. A change comes over that maggot-like creature. It rises to the surface, its skin splits and out comes a mayfly, easing its gauzy wings back and forth as if to pump the blood into new vessels. Then for a few brief hours it dances in the sun, mates, lays its eggs and falls to float and die on the surface and drift downstream to oblivion.

The banks of the chalk stream are at their most beautiful at mayfly time. Contented cattle, wither-deep in meadow grass, chew a lazy cud. The golden chalices of buttercups glow in the sun, the air is full of birdsong and the trees dressed in newly minted leaves. The water flashes silver-gilt as it hurries by, chuckling over the shallows, gliding slow and cool over the deeps.

Our mayfly is not alone, for myriads of them hatch at the same time and the length of the stream is a cloud of fairy shapes dancing over the water and grass, catching the sunlight and whirling in a mad kaleidoscope of colour. Up they go with a flickering of transparent wings, they hang a second and then parachute down, long thread-like tails turned upwards, then up they dart again, a million of them all at once, up and down until they bewilder the eye.

Suddenly they seem to tire of the game and all at once fall to settle on the grass which becomes a carpet of their greeny-brown bodies, each upcurled like a sickle, tail whiskers a-tremble. Then, as at a signal, up they rise and the mad whirling dance resumes, many mayflies locked together in an ecstasy of mating. They drop down and sit lightly on the water, depositing the first batch of countless eggs. Up and down they fly, laying another thousand at each landing until the fly is spent and can rise no more.

In droves they die and fall on the water, wings demurely closed, some flickering faintly and sending out little ripples from their dying bodies. To start with, their wings are upright but then, with a shiver first one falls, then the other and the dead mayfly lies like a crucifix and floats unresisting downstream. These elfin creatures are the true ephemerals, here today and gone tomorrow, the long preparation and then the final orgy of dancing, mating and dying all in the few short hours of a summer's day.

The adult mayfly is as succulent as it is plentiful and its sudden arrival in such bountiful numbers has a strange effect on the trout, and all the other fish for that matter. After a year of feeding choosily, rejecting this morsel in favour of that, the older and larger fish looking to the river bed rather than its surface for their food, suddenly they lose all caution and go mad. They are like the Israelites, starving one day and the next waking to find the ground knee-deep in manna.

Great fish which have not risen to a floating fly for a twelve-month, abandon their natural suspicion, rush up and roll on the surface like salmon, sucking and slurping at the bounty. They are carelessly ravenous, thrashing about in negligent gluttony close to the bank, the rings of their rises overlapping one another, the whole surface broken with silver flashes and the glimpse of dark nebs suddenly thrust out. "Those whom the gods wish to destroy they first make mad."

The angler has no more need of caution since even a careless cast will not 'put them down' for they have the fever upon them. Wherever his green drake or spent gnat – it matters little which fly he ties on – should fall, a fish is likely to rush at it with none of the usual circumspection which makes even a hungry trout look not twice but three times at tinsel and feather.

These are not your common or garden tiddlers, run-of-the-mill fish which on any other day would be worth stalking, but 4 and 5lb monsters of a size you never dreamed existed in this water. J. A. Froude, fishing the Ches, took two baskets of enormous trout when he caught the mayfly just right on a swollen stream. He stopped rather than abuse the opportunity but the old keeper reckoned that as long as he had known the river he had never seen so many large fish taken by one rod in a single day.

On noted mayfly rivers such as the Test they hatch in such myriad numbers as to be uncountable and many more than whole shoals of fish could eat. Their dead and dying bodies form a solid carpet, piling up in eddies and backwaters before being swept in a moving sheet steadily on and out towards the sea.

Not only trout capitalise on the feast. Grayling and coarse fish, chub, dace and roach take their share. They are slower to the rise than trout but there is plenty for all. Insect-eating birds flock to the table and swallows, martins, wagtails, warblers and finches hover and flicker, taking mayflies with audible snips of their beaks.

For all this orgy of gluttony there are so many insects that a great many live long enough to ensure the next generation. The successful ones will have laid their eggs which sink to the bottom. In time they become mayfly larvae and two years later they too will have their hour and rise and dance their desperate, brief whirligig in the summer sun.

53

Romany Morning

Every year they came, usually in late June. We heard them before we saw them, a clip-clopping of hooves toiling up the hill from the lower road, the children running out to watch. The gypsies were back, having come from goodness knows whence and, when they left, going who could guess where. Pluck up courage to ask one where he had been or was going and he jerked a blackened thumb over his shoulder, replying gruffly, 'back yonder' or 'pushing on west'. Locals who thought they knew, said they were on their way from the winter vegetable harvest in Lincolnshire down to the Vale of Evesham where they spent the autumn picking fruit.

The five gaily painted caravans moved steadily along the dusty highway, buckets hung below, nets of hay for the piebald horses tied on behind. The leading caravan was driven by a wizened old woman smoking a short clay pipe. She was dressed in long filmy skirts, grimy but colourful, with stout boots showing below and on top she was wearing an army combat jacket, complete with sergeant's stripes. She wore a faded rose in her long grey hair. A leash of broken-coated lurchers loped near the back wheel. As they passed they glanced at the bystanders, not the open look of honest dogs, but furtive, faces turned to the front, eyes swivelling under half-closed lids. They had the look of dogs which knew a thing or two.

The travelling tinker had a dog very similar. It trotted by his cart as he went his rounds. From his high position on the driving seat he could see over hedges and walls and spy a feeding rabbit or a hare in a form close to the boundary. He would rein in to walking pace and at a chirruped signal the dog slid like butter over the wall, surprising the rabbit by its sudden appearance. There was a short chase, a scuffle and a squeal and the dog, with its victim clamped in its jaws, glided back over the wall and took the rabbit to his master. The old man stowed it safely under the sacks on which he sat and resumed his normal pace. The gypsies' dogs looked cut out for much the same sort of work.

Their carts were works of art. Carved in scallops and knobs, painted yellow picked out in red, with a glimpse of a glass lamp shade from within and a dirty chimney stack poking from the top,  they were ancient in design, unchanged for centuries. The only nod to modern times were the rubber tyres which replaced the iron-shod wooden wheels.

They parked in an orderly row past the end of the village on some waste ground and, with the uncanny knack of making wherever they stop their home, they soon had a fire going and a line of washing spread across the top of a thorn hedge to dry. Grimy infants came out to play, running round the fire or sitting on the steps of the carts. They were thin, wiry and dangerous with black, curly hair and bright eyes. The slow, plodding youngsters of the village stood in a group for safety and, from afar, regarded them with a mixture or awe, envy and fear.

They tethered their horses in a row along the wide verge, each one attached to a long chain and a stake hammered into the ground. We were used to horses working the farms and pulling the milkman's cart but these were different. They were brown and

white in patches, like the maps that hung on the schoolroom wall, shaggy of mane and long of tail but all strong, well-made and bred as only gypsies can breed horses.

It was not often that they stayed for more than a few days but sometimes the men found work on a local farm and they settled in for two or three weeks. Then the School Board Man in his suit and bowler would call at the site and insist that youngsters of age should attend the local school. With reluctance some of them turned up and sat at the back, going through the motions, saying little, causing no trouble, learning nothing.

They were unlettered but they knew more of life and the ways of folk than our hobbledehoys would learn in a lifetime. The teachers bothered little with them knowing that they would soon be gone. They kept themselves to themselves and tolerated the imprisonment. If squabbling did break out it did well for the village boy to look to his safety for, when pushed hard enough, those boys, and girls too, would fight like wildcats.

The womenfolk did the rounds of the village houses. Knocking on doors they would proffer their embroidered cloths, clothes-pegs, which they made from coppiced hazel, or offer to read palms and tell fortunes. They stood on the doorstep proud and confident, their sloe eyes gazing straight ahead, earrings dangling, brown skin glowing after long days in all weathers. The village dames were flustered and uncertain how to react. Some bought through nervousness with a vague fear of the consequences should they demur, others through genuine kindness while the ones as tough as their own whalebone corsets sent them about their business.

It was open knowledge that they ran a long net by the squire's park one night and they strolled innocently about the fields with their long dogs delicately stepping alongside. While no-one actually saw it happen there was no doubt that the hare population suffered a few losses and there were certainly some nice smells coming from those blackened chimneys some evenings.

The keepers thought it wiser to look the other way than risk a confrontation. The travelling folk would be gone soon. One keeper wiser than the rest once arrived at their camp carrying a brace of hares he had just shot. He handed them over to the head man

and they chatted. None but they knew how that conversation went for certainly the keeper spoke of it to no-one. The next day he came with another hare and they chatted again. For some reason his was the only ground from which they stayed clear during their visits. They met with little enough kindness from 'normal' folk but when they did it was acknowledged.

In our isolated community they represented a threat. Travelling for us was local and by bicycle and yet they wandered the length of the land stopping where they wished and moving on when the mood took them. Not for them our comfortable, predictable lives, the same view, the same house and the same street to look at every day of our lives. They had seen things and places which we would never know, were not as us and were to be treated with the suspicion we reserved for the unconventional. They had rejected our way of life in favour of one more glamorous, but our suspicion was mixed with envy for deep inside we wished that we could do it too.

Suddenly one day they were gone. Early in the morning they harnessed the horses, backed them into the shafts and taking all they possessed, and sometimes a few things they did not, they set off along the dusty highway going we could not guess where. They left behind them surprisingly little rubbish, the blackened patches of their open fires and swathes of grass verge speckled with dung, cropped pale and bare by their horses. The carts moved out at that easy ground-eating pace which did not appear fast but if you kept it up it would take you many a mile before sundown. The long dogs took up their usual station, trotting servile but sly by the wheels.

They took with them their little bit of magic and whiff of danger. Their colourful ways were gone from our midst and we were left with the rural tedium of the daily round and the common task. As they faded round the bend and the dust of their passing rose and gently settled, they carried with them something of our own dreams and aspirations and they left us feeling strangely uncomfortable and somehow disturbed.

The feeling faded along with their dust and slowly life returned to normal. You could be sure that next summer the sound of hooves on the lower road would signal their return from wherever they had been.

Mailed Warrior

Down the green lane, across the hay meadow and hidden in a clump of trees beyond lies the carp pond. A century before it had been a duck decoy, one of those engines of destruction which took wildfowl by the thousand by the simple trick of luring them along a netted pipe by means of a foxy-looking dog. The birds pursued their old enemy not noticing that the pipe along which he had drawn them was narrowing and that it had curved away from the pond which now was out of sight. By then it was too late and they were flushed into the net at the end and sent off to market. The decoy at Lakenheath sent a ton of ducks to London every week and once there were more than seventy working decoys in the eastern counties.

That was long ago and the pond once so jealously guarded and lovingly maintained with banks thickly wooded the better to maintain its deadly quietness, is sunken in. The banks have collapsed, the grass and weeds once carefully mown are long and rank. The pipes have long gone but hunt in the nettles and you might discover a rotten, wooden stub standing like a broken tooth. Take the time to find a few more and trace their outline and you will rediscover the sweeping curves of the three pipes which once did such deadly work.

Now the acre of water lies quiet. As you approach you catch a glimpse through the trees of green ripples winking while the white flash of a moorhen's rump flirts by the lily pads. Find a place where there is grass rather than stinging nettles on which to sit and take your ease. The day has been as hot as August can produce but now the sun is swimming down in the west and losing its power to scorch. It is cooler here by the water and there is no one with you to share the tranquillity of a scene which is timeless.

Your ears become attuned to sounds more subtle than the bustle of the High Street you left twenty minutes ago and you can hear little rustlings in the brambles which overhang the water. Somewhere a moorhen croaks and there is a desultory burst of the summer song of a robin suddenly cut short, for August is not the month for bird music. With a flick and a dart of grey a sparrowhawk flashes over the water from behind you, zipping up at the last moment to top the hawthorn hedge yonder, and is gone. You look about you for the kingfisher but today he does not show.

The sun drops slowly until it is behind the high hedge and shadow falls across the pond changing its colour from lavender to lovat. Then, passing in the water at your very feet is a vision so fleeting and uncertain that you might imagine you had dreamed it – a great blue-black shadow shaped like a giant dumb-bell glides

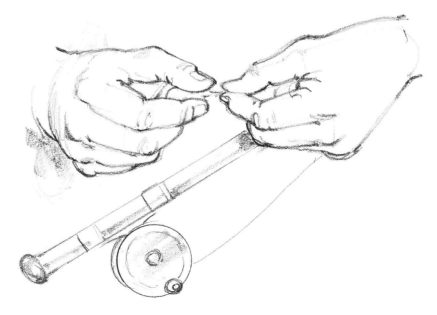

past. Your brain registers an impression of Norman chain mail, a vast dorsal fin and then a tail as wide as both your hands, which furls lazily, propelling the great fish forwards. Then it is gone leaving you rubbing your eyes, uncertain as to whether you had suffered an optical illusion.

You watch the place where you guess it now to be and a faint bow wave made by something like a miniature submarine ripples out to fade and die on the bosom of the water. It was no illusion but a carp. Coming to this conclusion, you are given spectacular proof that you are right. Without warning there is an eruption out in the middle and a fish the size and shape of a bag of potatoes heaves its bulk a yard out of the water. For a moment it seems to hang there defying gravity, droplets falling from bronze flanks, and then with a crash it falls on its side with an explosion and a wave which sets the bankside reeds rustling and vanishes into the depths whence it came.

You have started almost from your skin at this apparition, such an unexpected and dramatic intrusion into the quiet of the evening. You had heard rumours of carp in the old decoy pond but had no idea that they were so big. Few fished for them – only one old fellow from the village who came and went quietly in the evenings and early mornings. He said little, would give away no secrets and kept himself to himself. The carp were said to be hard to hook and harder to land due to the brambles which overhung the margin and the bed of lily pads into which hooked fish invariably made their first, unstoppable run. Once in that green underwater jungle they could not be extricated.

You decide to prove them wrong. The next evening you are there with your tackle and a bag of bread. Your gear is stout and hooks large, for these fish are the strongest that swim in British waters; even a salmon cannot match their first irresistible rush. You throw out flakes of bread for ground bait, impale a tempting piece the size of a golf ball on your hook and lightly cast out.

This is the waiting time. No carp angler is impatient. Those who hunt the real monsters might go many days or even weeks without a bite. They know that a cunning old carp will lie for an hour regarding the bait with a suspicious, piggy little eye, assessing the possibilities, suspecting a trap but tempted all the same. The over-eager angler who suddenly hauls it up to see how it is getting on does no more than teach an already wily fish another useful lesson. Next time it will wait even longer before taking and may well not do so at all.

Your bread has sunk to the bottom of the decoy pond. Light fades and some fish are moving for there are sucking sounds like a giant's kisses from beneath the lily leaves where a carp is taking insects off their undersides. There is a swirl on the surface and a small carp rises to a scrap of willow twig which it takes in its mouth and swims away with before spitting it out with a definitive puff.

The water is disturbed and muddy where you threw your groundbait, so fish are feeding, but carp have the knack of knowing which bread is attached to a hook and which is not. Now it is about as dark as it will get in high summer, one of those hot, velvety nights when nightingales sing in the thickets, moths blunder, mosquitoes whine their reedy song and an owl hoots far off in the vicarage elms.

You are about to reel in when something makes you stay your hand. Wisely you had left the bale arm off the reel having heard many tales of carp pulling whole rods into the water, often never to be recovered. The fish should feel no resistance when he takes. With a clutch at your heart you realise that the line is creeping out slowly and stealthily. You allow it to trickle over the back of your hand, definite movement there and the hairs prickle on the back of your neck. Somewhere down deep a fish has your bait in his mouth and is swimming slowly away with it.

It is a thrilling but disturbing moment. When do you strike? You are reminded of the old Chinese proverb to the effect that let him who hunts the tiger be sure he wants to meet it. It must be now. A decison made, suddenly resolute, you snap the reel handle, stand up and strike firmly. The rod bends into an impossible arch as though you had struck into a bag of sand. There is an eruption in the water and a great boil on the surface. The fish is up and running: you might as well have attached your hook to the tail-board of a runaway lorry, for no power on earth can stop it.

It is streaking out over the lake straight for the lily pads. You apply all the side strain your tackle will take, putting your shoulders into it. The fish seems to waver for a moment and half veers as if to miss the weeds, but it recovers and makes a determined dash into the middle of them and stops. All goes dead. You pull this way and that and suddenly with the sickening feeling well known to those who angle for big fish, the rod straightens and the line springs out and back over your head. No point now in secrecy and with your lantern you recover your tackle, running your hand down the line feeling for the hook. The stout wire which you have used to quell monsters in more open waters has been bent out straight.

Sadly you reel in and pack up. The old timer in the pub had been right. You had to be very good indeed or very lucky to land a large carp from the decoy pond. Large and obvious they might appear to the spectator but try to get one onto the bank to admire and photograph before returning it was a very different matter.

You have the consolation that at least you had one of the monsters on for half a minute and never would you forget that awesome power, that feeling of being attached to something stronger than you or your tackle. There had been others who had tried in that pond for the whole summer and had not so much as a take. You have to console yourself with that.

The next evening your footsteps somehow take you that way again. You have no fishing rod for you know when you are defeated. In your bag you have the remains of your bait from last night. You sit in your old spot, where the grass is trampled after your recent adventure, and cast your bread upon the waters. You have to wait very few minutes before a great mouth into which you could have slipped a tennis ball breaks surface and with a sucking sound engulfs half a slice. The fish sinks gently from sight and rises again to the next piece, another slurp and it too is gone.

These are ancient fish: who knows but they may have been fingerlings in the day when the old decoy was in full production. They know well enough what is and is not safe for them to eat. As the ancient in the pub was fond of remarking, 'No point in getting old unless you get crafty too'.

Fall of a Tyrant

Things were not well down on the lake. A passer-by might see only smiling ripples glancing in the spring sunshine, nodding sentinels of old willows bursting into bud round the margin, the dimples of rising rudd on the surface and moorhens flirting their black and white tails where the young lily pads were unfurling. Sheep grazed the grass down to the water's edge, the manor house stood red-bricked and mellow in the beeches, dreaming of lost Victorian greatness. It was as peaceful and pastoral a piece of old England as you could wish to find in a week of walking.

Pause a while and stand quietly by the stunted dogwood by the feeder stream and watch. You hear a gentle quack and a mallard duck shows briefly near the rushes. She looks about making sure she is alone, quacks once more and swims a few strokes out onto the bosom of the lake. Behind her comes a sprinkling of fluffy little balls of black and yellow which are her ducklings. There must be nine or ten of them, hard to count as they scuttle and scurry here and there, snatching at insects, racing each other for some especially tempting morsel. Let one stray too far and mother gives another quack, slightly more anxious with a note of command, and the wanderer comes scurrying back to the safety of the family.

It is a charming idyll and you watch enthralled as the duck leads her brood out onto the middle of the lake, the sun making her soft brown feathers glow. Her head turns this way and that, not feeding herself but watching for hawks, mink, cats, and busy with all the other worries which come with motherhood.

 With no warning Armageddon strikes. It happens in a split second but to the watcher it appears in slow-motion. The water bulges and breaks, there is a flash of a huge head all black, green and white, half a glimpse of raking teeth and a great eye as the water boils. Suddenly it is gone, only the ripples of that nightmare vision rolling, running, then trickling out to the margin where they die in the bankside reeds. There is one duckling less. The mallard gives a squawk of alarm, the surviving brood rush to her and she hurries back to the safety of the reed-bed on the far side, vanishing in the brown stems.

It was a pike of course, a big one for that shallow water, come in from the feeder stream and taking up residence, grown fat preying on the water voles, duck and moorhens. It looked above its head for food, turning to the shoaling rudd only when times were hard. For him, or rather her, for all large pike are female, this was harvest time and she meant to make the most of it. The sight of those little scuttling feet dodging hither and thither above was strangely exciting. Pike are often attracted to the limping spinner, the swimming frog or anything which moves erratically or jerkily within its field of vision. Usually they prey on sick or injured fish which also move spasmodically and trigger the predatory lust of old *Esox*.

Jem was the estate worker. In his time ploughboy, horseman, part-time gamekeeper and poacher, he could lay a hedge, set a row of 'taters, snatch a fish and catch and skin a rabbit in a way which made you blink. His coat was ragged and the colour of old moss, his cord breeches patched and muddy and his wellies turned down at the tops but his eye was as bright as a robin's and through half-closed lids there was little that escaped him. He had the skill, rare in a bustling age, of being able to stand motionless until it seemed that he vanished, fading and blending into the greens and browns of a rambling hedge or the shady corner of a stackyard where the elders grew.

He knew of the monster of the Hall pool and had seen it take young duck, sometimes quite large ones and more than once a full-grown moorhen had vanished within its maw. Jem felt the time had come to help Nature to balance herself. The pike could take one or two and welcome but this year she seemed to be obsessed with feathered prey and the pond's bird population was suffering.

He came down on a certain Wednesday in June armed with his piking tackle, determined to rid the world of the monster. His gear was not exactly Hardy's of Alnwick. It consisted of a cane rod inherited from his father which must have been at least eighty years old, a wooden centre-pin reel and a selection of accessories which he kept in a series of tobacco tins showing the names of long forgotten smoking mixtures, some of them popular in the trenches in the Great War. He kept it all in a battered, wicker basket which was older than he was. However, his touch was delicate and his knowledge of the quarry infinite. Many a time he outfished men equipped with all the modern technology of carbon fibre and electronic bite indicators.

He sat on the bank and assembled his gear, tying on a copper spoon which he himself had made and which had accounted for many a pike. The technique of centre-pin casting was almost lost in these days of the fixed-spool reel but Jem could do it in his sleep. The flash of copper flew through the air and plopped into the water on the far side. As a cuckoo burst out calling from the alders he began to reel in, pause, retrieve, speed up, slow down, the scrap of copper limping and fluttering through the green depths in a way which had lured many a monster to its doom.

Systematically he worked the pool from end to end, searching out the deep holes and sheltered lies under the reeds where a pike might lie. Then there came a quick jerk on his line and he struck. There was a brief pull then token resistance and he reeled in a pickerel of about a pound. Only a tiddler but there were far too many of them and it was better out of the water so he tapped it on the head and threw it into the hedge bottom. The monster remained sulky so Jem changed his tactics. He took a sprat from his basket and rigged up the end tackle known to anglers as a paternoster. He swung it out, let it sink and left it. The oily flavour might attract a big one for it was a well-tried and popular bait.

Even this failed and he returned home fishless. Next day he came back with a can of livebait caught from the pond behind his house. They were small roach and rudd and a pike like this might be lured by the real thing. Again his tackle swung out and the little roach, delicately impaled in a way which did not hurt it or impede its swim-ming, flashed and wheeled under the *Fishing Gazette* pike bung which did duty as his float. He landed another small pike and that was all. Again he went home defeated, an unusual thing in his angling career.

He lay in bed that night considering the problem. That fish had rejected spinner, live and dead bait, the three old faithful methods. Then it came upon him with a flash – he had been using traditional baits for a pike which had grown used to feeding in an unusual manner. It wanted its food up above swimming like a duckling or moorhen. He could lie there no more but in the small hours rose and went out with a lighted lantern to his shed. He rummaged about and came out with an old champagne cork: who had drunk the stuff Jem could not say except that it wasn't him. He had a length of valve tube for mending leaks in his bike tyres and this he cut into four pieces and bound them firmly with fuse wire to each end of the cork, creating the effect of four floppy legs like a frog. Finally, he threaded on a wire trace with a needle-sharp treble hook on the end and felt that he could do no more.

He was down again next morning with his invention. Once more he cast out and it plopped down on the far side. He took up the slack and began to reel in, the cork bobbing along, leaving a little wake behind it, its 'legs' trailing, flexing and straightening. He stopped it dead and started again, varying the speed and direction, zigzagging it back towards him. It looked as near as dammit, he thought, like a swimming duckling.

On the fourth cast it happened. The cork was halfway across the pool, stopping and starting, when the water erupted, that evil head showed for a moment, the cat's-claw teeth slashed and down it went, taking the lure with it. Jem struck like a marlin fisher, the old rod arching and creaking at every rickety joint. All held, the hooks were set and the pike bored away in a searing run which took it the length of the pool. Line screamed off the reel, the handle was a blur and Jem dare not interpose his thumb for fear of a nasty knock. The fish stopped and came back, Jem running back from the bank and reeling in as fast as he could to keep in touch.

Then the fish was out of the water, standing on its tail, 'tail walk-ing' anglers call it, shaking its head in a blur of foam in an attempt to throw out this troublesome nuisance it had taken. Jem dropped the rod tip for this was a dangerous moment but the hooks held firm. The fish ran shorter now, boring down to the depths, thrashing on the surface, sudden sharp runs, streaking out to the side but now growing weaker.

Suddenly, after five minutes, it was done, for even the biggest pike surrender suddenly. Slowly and on its side it allowed itself to be towed to the bank, energy spent, its best shot fired. This was another tricky moment and Jem had his net ready. Even then one desperate explosion of energy, a last ditch dash for freedom might have won the day, but the great head and slab side slid over the rim of the net until most of it was in. Jem dropped the rod, got both hands to the rim of the net, for he did not trust the handle, and hauled the fish out onto the grass.

The hook had barely penetrated that bony palate and his home-made spinner fell out onto the grass. The champagne cork was, as he recalled later, 'well chawed up'. The fish was a beauty, dragging down the notch on his spring balance beyond the 23lbs mark. Its tail, big as the sail of a boy's yacht, faded from green to orange brown; along its flank were rows of blotches fading to a belly as white as snow – a deadly camouflage as it lurked in ambush in the reeds. Its fins were perfect and undamaged, great sweeps designed to help the swift dash for prey. Its head was massive, that liquid eye as soft and gentle as a deer's but quite without pity or any emotion. The mouth was fearsome, a rat trap of needle teeth raking inwards; even its bony tongue, the roof of its mouth and the base of its throat were a thorn hedge of spikes.

Jem kneeled by the monster, in his hand the short, weighted club or priest, so-called because with it he would administer the last rites – a sharp whack on the base of the head. He enjoyed eating pike, which his missus cooked as well as anyone in the village, and one this size would be a feast indeed. Something made him stay his hand. He was as tough as they came but the thought of ending with one blow the life of such a noble creature which had taken many years to attain this size made him pause. The pike had committed no crime save to conflict marginally with man's interests; it deserved better.

Suddenly, a decision made, he dropped the priest back into his creel. He took the sack he used to line his bicycle basket, tore as much moss as he could find from the edge of the field and soaked it well in the pond. Tenderly he put the great fish on this damp bed and wrapped her up in it. The river lay but two hundred paces from the lake: she would be all right there, not many duck but lots of room to hunt and no end of 'rubbish' coarse fish for her to eat. She might even do him a good turn by mopping up the tiddlers which ate food which the bigger fish needed.

He cradled that great weight in his arms and set off at a smart walk. He found a place where he could approach close to the river's edge, lay down his load and unwrapped his prize. There was moss sticking to her flanks but that would soon wash off. He took her up, crouched down and lowered her head into the water, allowing her body to slide in after it, holding his hands beneath her to steady her. She paused a moment, gills working, tasting the flavour of new water, then gave a twist of her tail and was gone, sinking slowly out of sight into the green depths.

Jem watched for a moment, slowly straightened his back, wiped his hands on his trousers and tramped back to where he had left his tackle. He took down his rod, packed his gear and cycled slowly off down the towpath and home. It would not be baked pike but baked beans for tea but he did not care. It was better as it was.

As his shadow faded from the scene there was a gentle quack in the rushes. The mallard duck, followed by her three surviving ducklings, swam out onto the lake and began chasing insects. The rural idyll returned; peace reigned once more.

Singing Masons

Singing masons building roofs of shining gold...' – such a pretty line and what a felicitous description of a colony of honey bees. Coined by the Roman poet, Virgil, before the birth of Christ, it confirms that bee-keeping is one of the most ancient branches of animal husbandry. Bees have changed little since those days although our understanding of them has increased and continues to do so. Many of the poet's observations in the fourth part of his handbook for farmers, *The Georgics*, written during the first century BC, have the ring of truth.

Down at the far end of the orchard, top-heavy with frothing apple blossom, stands a row of hives – the old cottage type, not the modern, more efficient Nationals. A street of squat, white tenements, the grass round their entrances scythed short in order not to impede the residents' comings and goings. There stands old Arthur who has kept bees all his life. A stranger approaching silent and unseen from behind the hawthorn hedge might be excused for thinking that the old fellow was wandering in his wits and mumbling to himself. His lips are moving and sounds coming forth, but he is only doing what beekeepers through the ages have done, talking to his multitudinous charges.

Bees must be told the family secrets. When the old lady at the manor died her grieving husband went straight down to report the fact to his hives even before he informed the rest of the family. Arthur was one of those happy beekeepers blessed both with peaceable bees and a calm disposition so that he could handle them without heavy veiling and too much smoke. The odd puff subdued them to the extent that they would walk across the backs of his hands, up his arms and even settle in clusters on his face. They seemed to know that he meant them no harm and did not fear them, for, like many wild creatures, bees can detect human terror a mile off.

His movements were slow and gentle, no wild thrashing of the arms to create alarm, and when bees gathered too thickly on his forearms he would brush them off as gently as a man might remove a cobweb from his sleeve. However, let an intruder approach, a prowling dog or small boy blundering past on a bird-nesting expedition, and the workers sailed out to battle, giving no thought to laying down their lives to protect the colony. For a bee to sting, which it can do only once in its life, means losing a vital part of its anatomy so such an act of defiance is suicide. A skilled beekeeper might grow immune to stings, although to one or two people a single sting can cause serious illness or even death.

Bees show a community spirit and selflessness which hold lessons for modern man. On a day in midsummer in a dark cloud a swarm sallies out of the old hive. They have adopted a new queen, the old hive was overcrowded or in some way become unsatisfactory so the great army gorges itself for the exodus, for there is no knowing how long it will be before they feed again, and sets off to establish a new colony.

The earlier in the summer they swarm the better their chance of survival, of building up a food stock to see them through the hungry winter. An old rhyme runs, 'A swarm of bees in May is worth a load of hay: a swarm in June is worth a silver spoon: a swarm in July is not worth a fly'. A July swarm has missed the best of the harvest and will be hard put to lay down enough stores for the cold weather.

The swarm settles on a branch, the end of a gutter or anywhere almost at whim. There they hang like a misshapen football and the beekeeper who is quickly on the spot can take the lot. He needs a veil and gloves, for swarming bees can be tetchy, especially when they have been out some time and are growing hungry. He tries to take them after dark when they will be calm.

Holding a cardboard box beneath the cluster he gives a vigorous shake or cuts the branch with secateurs and down they fall with a thump, more like a single entity than 10,000 individuals. He takes the box home and props it against the entrance of an untenanted hive. One of the great sights of bee-keeping is to see the whole colony fan out and flow up the board and in, like liquid gold, until there is not one remaining. From inside the hive comes a purposeful buzzing for already they will be laying down the foundations of the comb which ensures the future of the tribe.

If the swarm is not captured it sends out scouts to all points of the compass to find a suitable place to colonise: a hollow tree, a hole in some thatch or the ruined chimney of some abandoned cottage. Those scouts are likely to die but they make the sacrifice for the common good. One will come back with news of a good place and the swarm will decamp straight there. Later scouts returning with good or bad tidings find the colony departed; it cannot be found again so they are doomed. The main thing is that the majority are safe.

The queen is the hub of this little universe. She lays every egg, tolerates no rival, is pampered by the workers and protected by them with no thought of their lives. Nurtured with royal jelly she has no need to fly, making only one important flight in her life. The new queen will fly up one sunny morning, higher and higher, followed by the male bees, the drones who do no work but are kept

fed and comfortable for this one day. The drones follow the queen as she rises and one by one they drop back exhausted. When there is only one left who by a process of elimination is the strongest and therefore of the sturdiest stock, the queen mates with him and from that union springs the eggs which ensure the future of the hive.

After this the drones are abandoned to their fate, their usefulness over. No longer do they have any contribution to make to the well-being of the hive. They are left out of the hive with no skills nor inclination to forage for themselves until the jaws of the workers, starvation or the first frost of winter kills them off.

If the queen is the fountain-head, the workers are the fabric which binds the colony together. They spend their short lives foraging and ferrying nectar from flower to comb, laying down stores which will keep hunger at bay in the winter. Miraculously they can travel three miles and find their way unerringly home, but move the hive ten yards in their absence and they are lost.

The workers keep the hive clean, repel intruders, feed the grubs of the next generation and, most important, look after the queen, clustering round her in the cold, fanning her with their wings when hot and seeing to her every need. Every act they perform is for the common good with no thought of self; everything they do is for the survival of the colony. Workers wear themselves out gathering and storing food they will never eat. They die defending the hive against enemies.

My own experiments at bee-keeping were not marked by success. I had a single fourth-hand hive of the old-fashioned, cottage type and took my swarm which had settled on a twig of whitethorn. I went at night when they would be peaceable and, with layers of veils and gloves stout enough to protect a welder, I snipped the twig and they crashed down into my cardboard box without demur. I was surprised at how heavy they were. Next morning they ran up into my hive and settled down.

The middle of the agricultural fenland was short on flowers. Cereals and sugar beet were not a rich hunting ground for honey seekers. David from the farm up the road would take his hives to bean fields and young oilseed rape, his open pick-up truck sur-rounded by a cloud of bees as he drove from place to place. I did not possess David's resourcefulness, his energy nor his truck.

For a short while I shared in the great pleasure and contentment there is to be had from caring for bees. To remove the roof, give a few puffs of smoke and watch them busy with their affairs was soothing and strangely cathartic. To stand a short distance from the entrance and see them coming and going, meeting briefly as they crossed, sometimes performing the delightful bee dance, by which an incomer will indicate the precise location of a rich foraging ground, was a beautiful way to while away an hour.

However, there was not enough food to sustain them, then a savage October gale blew the hive over and in the end my amateur bunglings were not enough to save them. Maybe my queen was old and past her best and not able to lay enough eggs to keep up the numbers. Whatever the reason, for all their incredible powers of survival my little kingdom died out. I made one unsuccessful attempt to replace them and then abandoned apiary to men wiser and more skilled in the great art.

A good hive will yield between 80 and 100lb of pure honey. The flavour and texture will vary depending on the flowers the bees have been working. Heather has a delicate flavour as does field bean whereas oilseed rape has a tendency to crystallise in the jar. All honey is valued for its health-giving powers. The honey taken must be replaced by liquidised sugar which will see the bees through the hard times. The keeper checks during the winter to top up the supply and make sure his charges are not going hungry. His heart warms to see one or two out on the dancing board on the first sunny days of spring, testing the temperature and beginning to think about the busy times to come.

Honey bees will defend their hive to the death against those who wander too close but some strains take less provoking than others, some of the imported continental bees being especially ill-tempered, not to be approached without full protection. Others are placid and slow to anger. Some things will irritate the most easy-going bee. They tend to be irritable in thundery weather, do not like people with alcohol on their breath, who sweat or display fear and they react badly to loud colours. For all their stout defence they are strangely tolerant of some interlopers. They will see off a wandering dog but a mouse is not uncommon as a lodger in the hive and the bees seem to leave it alone. It creates havoc eating the brood comb and can destroy the whole colony unless dealt with. Beekeepers fit a mouse guard to the entrance to keep the rascals out.

Other disasters can strike. Insect-eating birds learn that here is a rich source of food and they hang about the hive entrance picking off the workers as they come to and fro. Far worse is some terrible scourge or plague such as foul brood which will affect a colony and spread rapidly. Ministry inspectors do the rounds checking hives to ensure that they are plague free, recording each case of infection as meticulously as though it were an outbreak of foot-and-mouth disease in cattle. Infected hives and bees must be burned to prevent spread, surely the most heartbreaking thing any beekeeper can experience.

Those folk who spend their lives tending living creatures are inclined to be gentle and placid, slow to anger and philosophical in their ways. The excitable, short-tempered and irascible are too impatient to form easy relationships with livestock and should seek more suitable pastimes. Above all the virtues, the beekeeper requires calmness. Arthur is typical of the breed, large and slow, a man of few words as, straw-hatted he stoops over his hive, peering at his charges within, murmuring pleasantries to them, noting the queen where she sits surrounded by her courtiers, seeing the workers sailing in, their sacks stuffed with nectar, furry bodies powdered with yellow pollen. From them all comes a deep-throated, contented humming. His ear would be quick to detect a change of note which shows that their mood was changing.

He is king and god of a vast population of subjects. He tends them and works in partnership with them for they would not tolerate exploitation. He governs their lives as a benevolent dictator, for self-sufficient and resourceful though they be, a kindly human hand eases some of life's difficulties.

Would that those who have in their hands the running of the great nations of our own world were so gently and wisely disposed: our troubles as a race would be few.

Tarka's Return

It lacks but half an hour to darkness. The river glides by, a dimpled pattern of hammered pewter ripples, eddies under the bank and the gentle swaying of reeds caressed by the current. I sit quietly on an old straw bale near the margin; it was left over from the winter feeding of pheasants. Our barn owl drifts by, a white moth wavering and floating. It pauses for a moment and hovers over my upturned face and stares down wondering what this strange moon-like shape might be. He passes on. A pair of mallard quack somewhere and a moorhen clucks. Rabbits come out from the hedge, hop, chase and pause to nibble the new grass.

It is the special time 'twixt light and darkness when Nature stirs herself. The night creatures come out and those of day prepare for rest. This is when a buck steps out of a thicket, a salmon rises or a spring of teal comes zipping round in the gloaming to land lightly with a splash.

I am about to rise and depart for the air grows chill and it is almost dark but then a new sound floats across the river. There are few noises on my own patch which I cannot identify, the crazy trilling of the grebes, stuck-pig shriek of water rail, water vole rustle and rabbit scream, but this is a new one. It is a long liquid whistle like the sound of a distant train coming through a tunnel. I watch and then down the stream comes a V-shaped ripple, at its point a blunt, bullet head so clear against water glint that I glimpse a large round eye and a frieze of stiff whiskers.

It is an otter, never before seen by me but instantly recognisable: it could be nothing else. As I watched it dived, a smooth, oily movement, sinuous and slick. Then it was gone and I saw it no more although a few moments later I heard that fluted whistle from further downstream.

All that was almost fifty years ago and I had not seen one since – until last week that is. Almost at the very same spot once more I saw an otter running briefly along the shelf where bank meets water and then slipping like butter down the throat of the pool and vanishing, although I watched for many minutes in the hope of seeing it again. The otter had returned after an absence of half a century, its numbers still sparse, its restoration to our waterways tentative but it had a toe-hold.

Those wilderness years had seen it fall on hard times. Otter hunting had rightly been banned although it was rare that the hunt ever caught one. The real enemy was the pollution of our waterways by detestable industrial and domestic effluent. Riparian disturbance, caused by heavy angling pressure and ignorant fishery managers who saw otters as threats to their livelihood, all contributed to the otter fading and then vanishing from most river systems.

The otter is a charming creature. A member of the *Mustelidae* family which includes weasels, stoats and badgers, it is beautiful and intelligent. Anyone who has been privileged to see a family of otters at play would confirm this. They make slides down the river bank and mother and cubs will play like so many children. They clamber up to the top of the slide and skitter down to plop in the water only to scramble out and up again to repeat the game. The slide becomes greasy and polished by the passage of otter bottoms and the fun is fast and furious. Slick brown bodies mingle in a blur of frenzied activity, sliding, splashing and scrambling. Let the mother catch the sound of a rustle in the reeds or the whiff of human scent and she gives a low, warning whistle. Instantly there is silence, every head up and listening and, as if by magic, they vanish.

In rocky rivers there are what are known as otter altars – slabs of

flat rock worn smooth by the passing of not hundreds but thousands of otter feet during countless generations. These favourite places are used by otters as tables and there they drag their fish, eels, crabs or lampreys and crunch them up.

Otters will migrate many miles following watercourses down to the sea, living on the shore for a few weeks before moving again into fresh water. Some of their routes are as old as the Romans for, like badgers, they are creatures of ancient pathways. Several otters have met their fate travelling up befouled waterways in the north of England through the heart of the industrial wasteland. They did not go there by choice but were following the instinct which took their ancestors that way when the streams were bubbling mountain rills, long before the chemicals and slums murdered the waters. It is a fair bet that otters will again swim up them when the industrial conurbations have passed away.

Otters mark their passing with deposits of spraint, their droppings – black, prickly with fish bones and smelling of fish paste. They have none of the rank odour of the fox, being clean animals. Web-footed tracks and spraint are appearing again in places where they were unknown for a human lifetime. Their food is not exclusively fish or crustaceans. They will conduct raids inland quite far from the water where they feel most secure. They will take a straying hen or maybe a pheasant off a nest and sometimes young rabbits, which they can surprise and catch. On the river they might take a grebe or moorhen and snatch a sitting mallard.

There are many who say that far from being an enemy of fisheries an otter can be a boon. Its favourite food is eel and eels take a great many young fish and trout and salmon eggs by the thousand. To see an otter wrestling with a 4lb eel is quite a spectacle with much threshing about and entwining by that slippery body but the otter has it firmly by the head and there is no escape. It will also hunt out weak fish which are no benefit to the water and also take the old cannibal trout which have taken to a life on the bottom. These are fish which no fly will tempt and they devour the eggs and fingerlings of their descendants.

The otter makes its nest or holt under the massive bole of a fallen waterside tree, where winter floods have hollowed out a

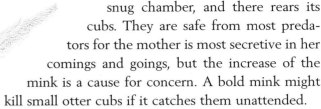

snug chamber, and there rears its cubs. They are safe from most predators for the mother is most secretive in her comings and goings, but the increase of the mink is a cause for concern. A bold mink might kill small otter cubs if it catches them unattended.

The tentative return of our favourite water creature is due to two main factors. First the National Rivers Authority (NRA) has taken strenuous measures to clean up polluted waterways. Salmon swim up the Thames along with many other fish which would have been impossible twenty years ago. Other poisoned streams are being returned to a degree of purity which can support wildlife. There is still a long way to go but there has been a significant improvement.

Phillip Wayre with his Otter Trust ran a programme of captive breeding and reintroduction. This took some time to take effect but due to his persistence and patience it began to bear fruit. There can be little doubt that many of the otters making a gradual return are direct descendants of that stock. Riparian owners have been alerted and educated and they keep their banks quiet, prevent angling on sensitive stretches and have made artificial holts from piles of logs to encourage otters to breed.

Once again it has become possible to sit quietly of an evening watching the sun go down and know that while it is still unlikely, for these are early days of recovery, it is not impossible that one day a long, low, liquid whistle will float to your ears in the bosky dusk along the quiet stream.

Autumn

Now comes the busy time for the countryman. There is a hint of anxiety about his chopping of logs, his garnering, gathering, storing and pickling. The air is mild, the evenings golden and the dawns misty, but hard times are coming. Farmers cut the corn and patient horses pulled heaped carts up the lane, while in the stackyard the threshing tackle hummed and the traction engine shimmered hot with the perfume of warm oil as it jigged back and forth.

Folk come up from the fields and to the church for harvest thanksgiving and after that the horkey, a more ancient and pagan celebration. The shotgun is taken down and oiled, and sunburned men march the cracking stubbles and shoot into the covies and at the lolloping hares; everything they bag they eat, for nothing goes to waste. The angler takes home pike, eels and perch, while the housewife makes jams and chutneys and lays a great store of goods for the hungry winter. The church bells ring out their brazen message of hope, the pub landlord draws the first pint of the evening while leaves on the churchyard limes grow yellow at the edges and the swallows depart.

Then one night the wind changes and we lay abed and shiver, thinking of the things done and undone as cruel winter on steel-shod feet creeps stealthily up from the fen.

Shock-Horse Boy

It is August and lacks an hour to dawn. Mist writhes in the hollows and lingers down by the byre. The dawn chorus is a wild carolling, the throaty cooing of woodpigeons from the elms laying down a bass line for the contralto of the blackbirds and thrushes, the treble of wren and great tit, with intermissions from the barnyard cockerel and a broken-voiced cuckoo outstaying his welcome and thinking it was time he was off to warmer lands. There was no other sound, for the inescapable drone of the motorway lay far in the future. There were but three cars in the whole village; the doctor and the vicar had Morris eights and the squire a Riley.

The sky was pale pink and it would be another scorching day. Then, from far off, came a new sound, a huffing and panting suddenly strenuous then quiet. Sometimes the clanking of a chain came on the breeze and then a gentle, double hoot as soft as a tawny owl in a hollow oak. It grew louder: I knew what it was and was up and out of bed, shivering and skipping on the cold lino, pulling on shorts and jersey and those big boots with tabs at the back, out of the kitchen door into dewy grass, through the shrubbery and down to the lane.

It was threshing time and today the tackle was coming from the next village to set up in the barnyard opposite our house. The driver had been up before dawn firing his boilers, making an early start so that he would have the whole day to manoeuvre his gear into position, an operation of great skill and complexity. For me it was a high spot of every year, each moment to be savoured and re-lived in the dull days of winter.

The rumbling grew louder until round the bend at the bottom of Church Lane crawled the traction engine towing behind it the great, pink threshing drum and behind that the elevator, all linked together by a series of bolts and shackles strong enough, it seemed

to me, to hold an ocean liner. Iron-grey smoke billowed and now the machine was level with me, a poem of polished copper, squirting steam, dripping taps and the scent of hot brasswork. The great iron wheels crunched little stones on the road for this was a leviathan, a behemoth of a machine, the most powerful thing I had ever seen.

The turn into the farm gateway was tricky. It was narrow with pillars of stone on either side which would not allow for error. To back that lot out of a tight place would be impossible so it had to be right first time. Suddenly the grimy man spun his steering wheel, chains under the iron belly of the machine tugged round the front wheels and, so slowly that he was barely moving, he inched the engine then the drum and finally the elevator through that impossible gap with inches to spare on either side. The top of the elevator brushed the overhanging tree and quite a large branch broke off and came swishing down. It was prettily done.

It was full daylight now and having trundled up the length of the stackyard he eased to a halt, climbed down, leaving his engine hissing like a bag of snakes, and unscrewed his thermos flask which he kept in a canvas bag slung on the back of his perch. Shire horses in the yard tossed their heads, snickered and whinnied watching with nervous interest for their busy time was here too. Other folk materialised from cottages and barns, the blacksmith wiping his hands on an oily rag, the farm foreman in a tweed coat and leather gaiters as shiny as conkers. The first farm workers swung into the gateway on their bicycles, dockey bags on their backs, old tweed caps pulled well down.

Most of the day was spent in setting up the tackle for a start next morning. The engine was unshackled, the elevator manhandled into position, the drum shunted, pushed and pulled inches at a time until it stood in line and just the right distance away. Finally the engine was jostled back and forth until it completed the triumvirate. Then the belts were attached, thick welts of iron-hard webbing rolled out and lifted over polished driving wheels and the great flywheel of the engine itself. An inch or two back to take up the slack, not too little, not too much for there must be a bit of give.

When all was in position to the satisfaction of the grimy man, great wedges of wood were jammed under the iron wheels to prevent movement. The green canvas tarpaulin was unroped and the engine slipped into gear. Slowly the flywheel revolved, gently the drum began to throb, everything turning at quarter speed, checking for final adjustments or noises which suggested internal troubles. Finally he built up steam, threw the throttle and the drum whirred, the elevator clacked round, belts scythed and wheels spun. All was ready. He shut off steam, climbed down again armed this time with a giant grease gun and spent the rest of the afternoon crawling about pumping grease into every nipple until it oozed blue and yellow from the joints.

Others had not been idle. Pitchforks were counted out and leaned in a corner. A mountain of hessian sacks were laid in readiness, sack-barrow wheels oiled and the pink tumbril carts checked for damage, harness oiled and horses given an extra feed. Tomorrow would be a busy day. Two carts full of sheaves had been fetched from the field down Station Road where 20 acres of stooks of bearded barley stood like the wigwams of an American Indian village.

The next morning was golden and the day would be hot, as were they all in the summers of youth. First to rise was the grimy man, firing his boiler with a handful of dry sticks and some knobs of coal. The horseman was tending his charges, feeding, then harnessing them and hissing his soothing, horseman's lullaby. One by one they were linked to the carts and patient and gentle they stood shifting their feet, tossing their heads and chasing the last oat round the bottom of the nosebag.

The engine was warming up, black coal smoke belching from the tall chimney with the brass band round the top. Men took pitchforks and stood under the elevator, others hooked coomb sacks under the chutes round the drum and brought up the sack barrows. The scene was set, ready for the entry of the star of the show – the Man in the Leather Apron.

This lofty individual was my hero, the man I most wanted to be. He occupied centre stage and, conscious of his position, mounted the ladder with slow dignity and climbed onto the top of the

drum. He fastened the straps of the apron and took out his knife, sharp enough to shave with. He was the man who fed the drum, the lynchpin of the whole operation, and to me only a step below the Almighty.

The pitcher stood on the load of sheaves on the cart and lightly flicked up the first one to the Man in the Leather Apron who stooped, lifted it, nicked the string with his knife and fed the corn evenly into the drum. It went in with a whoosh, he stooped for another and suddenly the day had started. The engine jogged back and forth, the drum throbbed, dust rose and hovered in the still air. The golden straw came walking up the elevator and tumbled over the end to be forked from one man to another to make the base of the great stack. Hessian sacks belched dust for 16 stones of rich grain was spewing into each. For wheat it would have been

18. The sack dropped the weight, the chute clanged over and sack number two began to fill.

The full sack was tied at the neck with a special knot, hauled onto the sack barrow, wheeled across the yard and up a sloping plank into the barn where another man lugged it into position. Every second sack he would wind up to shoulder height on his winder, balance that great weight across his shoulders and drop it lightly on top of sack number one. By the end of the day he had serried ranks of them standing neatly like grenadiers. Try getting a man to heft 16 stones these days.

The grimy man threw on more coal, topped up the water and wielded his oil can. Smoke mingled with dust and the perfume of hot metal I had sniffed the day before. Chaff rose and drifted, men scurried here and there, straw whirled down to be forked and above it all, oblivious of the organised chaos below, the Man in the Leather Apron bent, straightened, nicked the string – always at the knot, for a good pitcher presented the sheaf knot uppermost – and in went another sheaf. When he had a handful of strings he would tie them in a bundle to the rail which surrounded his eyrie. At the end of the day it was festooned with bundles like scalps hanging on a lodge pole. The strings were recycled to tie up the sacks.

I was a small part of this operation for I was one of six shock-horse boys, known in Norfolk as 'Hold-ye Boys'. My job was to ride an empty horse and cart down Station Road and in at the field gate to join the other team, those who pitched and loaded the carts. Waiting my turn I would lead my horse, pulling a full cart back up the lane to the stackyard, passing another empty one coming down. The patient horses were gentle but so strong. I had to jump quite high to reach the bridle and watch out to see that they did not stand on my toe or slow down to snatch mouthfuls of vetch from the verge. Plodding up the hill was one thing but going down empty you had the chance to ride, sitting on the raves facing that enormous bottom and swishing tail, as flat out at a mile an hour down we went, feeling like the driver of a Western stage coach escaping pursuing Indians.

I was paid 10s a week for this but I would willingly have done it for nothing. The farmer came into the yard to see how things were going and talked to the grimy man. He put his hand in a corn sack and smelled and caressed the sample holding it up to the light and testing it with his fingers.

Then it was dockey time, the fenman's mid-morning break. The wheels eased, the flailing belts slowed until they were barely moving, dusty, brown-armed men came down the ladder from their stack now grown tall. The engine hissed and steamed, no smoke only shimmering hot air over the funnel now, as we sat round in the barn eating our sandwiches. On my first day they tied me up in a coomb sack for my lunch hour. This was their crude but harmless initiation for the newest shock-horse boy. Dusty and dishevelled and close to tears I emerged to set off down the lane again with the latest empty.

So it was, day after day, all that golden and endless summer long ago. Horses plodded, the Man in the Leather Apron bent and straightened like an automaton, never rushing, never pausing, sacks shuttled back and forth, stacks grew, were completed and we moved to another space to start the next. We finished the barley and went on to the wheat which had been ripening in the shock. This time the man in the barn had to heft 18 stones at a time, one

every minute of the day. A mass of dead weight welded to his back, he tottered across the floor to drop it on its fellow. Folk stopped to watch, for the harvest was important to all village people. A good one meant bills paid and general prosperity.

Then it was evening and knocking-off time. The sun sank in blood, another hot day tomorrow. The engine let off steam with a blast, the fire box cooled while the tarpaulin was roped down over the drum. Freed of harness, their labours over, the horses galloped round and round their corral, rolling on their backs and kicking their great hooves in the air like overgrown children let off school. Men cycled home, light faded, silence fell and a barn owl came out like a yellow moth and hunted for mice round the new stack.

None of us knew that we were part of a dying era of agriculture. Where the stackyard stood and the owl hunted, where the smithy was and the old barn, where generations of sun-browned men sweated and worked to bring home the harvest is now a housing estate of pseudo-Georgian 'residences' occupied by commuters who work away from the village. The owl, the grimy man and even the Man in the Leather Apron have gone to their long home for, eheu, that was almost half a century ago.

Fate was to hold a curious twist for me. At a country fair where I was commentating there was a steam engine, drum and elevator threshing a stack for the modern urbanites to gawp and wonder at the quaint old ways. Knowing my childhood admiration for the Man in the Leather Apron, the owner invited me to take his place for a while.

With trembling fingers I tied the apron strings and mounted the ladder. The drum seemed smaller than it had been all those years ago but a dream had come true. The sheaf was pitched to me, I stooped, cut the string and fed the golden stalks into the gaping maw of the drum. They went in with a whoosh, a sound which brought me close to tears and spoke eloquently of times past, the sweet old times of childhood which would not come again.

Muir Cock

The very word moor has a desolate sound to it. There is something mournful there, a touch of the Brontës and of desolation, moaning winds, bleakness, a place where the sun never shines. Your mind's eye shows sheep-speckled slopes and heather which runs on to a purple horizon. There are peat hags to trap the unwary, you half remember 'O' level geography exams and the term 'marginal grazing' comes to mind.

There is just such a swathe of real estate somewhere high in the Yorkshire Dales which is all those things but many more. As well as the sheep, heather and desolation it is the home of a few

scattered covies of grouse and it is because of them that every year a strange and disparate group of individuals comes together in August to tramp that wild place in the hope of a shot at them.

For fifty-one weeks of the year those folk lead ordinary, prosaic lives but get them talking about their own little bit of heaven and their eyes sparkle, their talk becomes animated and the reminiscences come rushing out. Memory dulls the pain of leg-aching tramping without a shot, of rain which slants up the hills and into your face, of wearisome hauls up slopes which seem to go on for ever. They are more keen to recollect their first grouse, their first driven grouse, their first right and left, the first shot of a son or a friend, any and each of them an excuse, as if one were needed, for a celebratory dram.

They might speak of braving the mosquitoes and lying out in the tussocks by the tarn for a mallard, the boggy hole found by following the telephone posts up the hill, the one to which they staggered with buckets of barley but which produced very few duck. It might be the black and white magpie blur of a rising blackcock – a rarity for us – flapping heavily from the bog cotton and rising to gain height and speed, curling down the line of guns. Usually it is missed, for blackcock fly faster than you think. Then there is the ecstasy of recrimination, the agonised wish for a second chance as the bird flees unscathed and two fruitless shots are spent.

That sad and wild place, so easily glanced at through a windscreen and dismissed as bereft of life, is home to many creatures as well as red and black grouse. Redshank ring their tinkling bells in spring and snipe drum. Curlew cry their sad calls, peregrines arch across the heavens, hen harriers quarter the ground like setters, short-eared owls, kestrels, merlins, linnets and pipits all live there in the company of great green and brown frogs and lizards which bask on warm rocks.

Swaledale sheep run, stop, stare with yellow eyes, cough, stamp and sneer before dashing away again. There are dogs there too, the Border collies which herd the sheep streaking like chips of black and white up the hill which so slowly we climbed earlier. These dogs stop, crouch, run nose to ground and are so obedient to whistle and shout that they put our gundogs in the shade. Wiry shepherds wrest a living from that harsh place, men hewn from granite, skin like leather and impervious to the weather. In old coats tied round the middle with string and a rain drop pendant on each red ear, they stride the moor tirelessly following their ancient calling.

They have the time for a friendly word in the morning when they pass with their buckets on the way to feed the cows, and we bless them for the days when they predict fine weather or report having seen lots of grouse up the hill. Whether or not they are right on either count is immaterial: they are being friendly and raising our spirits with the instinctive courtesy you find in country people.

We have our own dogs of course and we love them dearly. Great soft Labradors, lively springers and sometimes the treat of an old-fashioned bird dog, a pointer or setter. They do their best to get in the way, keep us awake with their barking and occasional skirmishing, make messes on the grass verges and wolf down great bowls of food mixed with black pudding left over from breakfast, the same black pudding which everyone ordered but found they could not face when it appeared on the plate. We forgive them their faults and each man secretly feels his dog to be not only the best one on the moor but the best in the whole wide world.

The lynchpin which holds together the strange assortment of humans and dogs and the great purple expanse of the moor is the cottage crouched at its foot. Five hundred years old, with damp walls many feet thick, it had once been the home of a shepherd, a man who walked those same hills which had changed little since his day. There are two main rooms downstairs, the lounge and the dining room. The furniture has seen better days but it is homely and comfortable and a roaring coal fire makes it snug once the walls have dried out. There is a cupboard which does duty as a bar

to which every visitor is expected to make a contribution in kind.

Upstairs are three large bedrooms full of bunks. There were times when more than thirty people slept there and one night we topped the forty mark. Bodies lie this way and that in sleeping bags like scattered pine cones on the floor. They sleep behind the door, behind as well as on the sofa, on the landing and below the row of coat hooks festooned with an array of waterproof coats, gun slips, hats and game bags. Every morning a miracle worker in the kitchen produces a full English breakfast for everybody.

Boots are pulled on, bags packed, guns checked and cartridges counted. You do not expect many shots but it is a long way from home if you happen to run out. We assemble at the sensible time of ten o'clock on the slabs in front of the cottage, listen to the briefing which never varied in twenty years and set off up the hill. One notorious slope was named by us Heart Attack Hill. It is long and steep and when you had breasted it and believed you had triumphed, there is another hill in front of it and another one after that.

We line out at the bottom and set off up and away turning to glance back to where the road snakes far below us up the valley. Passing grey stone sheep folds built when the first Charles was on the throne, we trudge through the cotton grass, conserving energy and taking the line of least resistance.

At last after a few stops for a breather we find ourselves at the top, on the plateau and in front of us the promised land, the purple bloom of the heather moor stretching to the horizon. If there is to be a grouse it will be here for they eat heather to the exclusion of everything else. From far off comes the glottal chortle of an old cock grouse, 'go bec, go bec, bec-bec-bec', running off into a throaty chuckle. You are encouraged to discover that there is at least one there.

The line which has grown ragged on the long haul up is straightened and off we go, wading though the heather from which pollen flies like talcum powder, dogs walking to heel or bustling in the cover in front. Just when one foot is deep in a peat hag, you are struggling for purchase with the other and your gun is waving wildly in the air, there is a dry rustle of wings and a covey rises close in front, fleeing off round the contour with throaty chuckle. You mount the gun, blot out a bird and pull. With luck there is a puff of white feathers running and trickling over the woody tops of the heather and your first bird of the season falls to bounce once

and lie still. Your dog has it back in a moment.

You stroke the richly patterned plumage, admire the feathery feet and marvel that such a bird can survive in that hostile place, through the savagery of a northern winter when the snow lies many feet deep and the wind screams as sweet as a razor across the wastes. Success puts a new bounce in your step and there are other shots from up and down the line. Everyone stops while a bird is picked and you take your ease on a heathery tussock.

So through the day, pulling up your collar at a sudden rainstorm, stopping for a break at lunchtime, swapping stories, sprawling in the sun, sipping at a can of ale and nibbling a cheese sandwich. Not for us bulging hampers brought up on ponies by well-groomed servants as in the old days. Meanwhile the sun chases great cloud shadows across the bottom of the valley, stones old as time itself stand lichen covered like petrified moss troopers, the stream burbles and the world is at peace.

By the time normal folk are having tea, we have meandered here and there, back and forth in the good heather, up and down the

less productive white moor, always with the hope of a grouse when least expected, a springing covey or an old singleton. Then it is time to come down, losing the high ground, descending into the realm of motor cars and the dwellings of saner people. Back at the cottage, feet aching, blisters throbbing gently, we sprawl on the same slabs on which we had stood so full of resolve seven hours earlier and gaze up through half-closed lids at the purple hills of which an hour ago we had been a part. A dozen brace of grouse hang in the old cart shed, a gin and tonic is in the hand so it is hard to imagine a group of folk more at ease with themselves and the world.

Then comes the queue for the one shower before the short trip up to the highest pub in the whole of Merry England where we rub shoulders with shepherds, hill walkers and an army of strange and ancient ghosts which whisper at the windows and cluster round the stone ingle. Back at the cottage an enormous steak and kidney pie is waiting, after which we put the world to rights over a nightcap until it is time for each to seek his own little patch of floorboards and sleeping bag ready to repeat the same mixture on the morrow.

On the last morning we go home, dispersing one by one, losing ourselves and each other in the wild threnody of the motorway system, rejoining what less fortunate people are pleased to call 'the real world'.

The memories remain intact except now and then when you are not certain whether or not your adventure had been a dream. The story-telling, the mass singing to the accordion, the jokes, lying in suspended animation in the heather at lunchtime, forcing tiring legs up just one more incline before the good heather and then the explosive magic of a whirring covey rising at your feet. Such should all sporting shooting be, birds hard earned, company treasured, the place paradise.

So when the talk comes round to moors, as if ever it would in the run of normal conversation, and others think vaguely of bleak, untenanted and weary miles of nothing much, I may be excused if a smug look steals across my face. I at least know better.

95

Harvest Home

Of all the seasons in the farming calendar the corn harvest used to be the most important. Not so now when a giant combine travelling faster than a man can trot gobbles up a whole farm in a week. A computer in the air-conditioned cab tells the operative (no longer a farm worker) should half a dozen grains spill out of the back. The harvest of childhood lasted for quarter of the year – the early barley cut in July, on to the wheat and well into autumn and threshing time.

The corn was cut with a binder hooked onto the back of a Fordson Major tractor. A decade before it had been a pair of horses. One man sat on the tractor steering round the shrinking square of corn, his mate perched on the tin seat on the machine, hanging onto the handles for dear life. He was there as much to shout a warning to the driver when the string broke or to leap off to knock over a rabbit as serve any serious agricultural function.

The binder rattled, blades shimmied back and forth and the stalks fell gently, lay on the canvas and shuffled up towards the magic which was the knotter. How man could make a gadget which tied a perfect knot time after time was a marvel of high technology in those days. Then with a flick of a three-fingered steel hand the sheaf rolled over and fell out onto the stubble.

It was important that the sheaves should not lie long enough to become dew soaked so they were shocked as soon as possible. Shocking or stooking is the propping up of the sheaves, one against another, in a short row like a line of wigwams. Shocks ran in ranks across a field so that the cart which was to collect them later could work in straight lines. A team of sun-bronzed men and women would spend day after day at this task. It looked easy and the sheaves flew so lightly from the hands of experts, but when I tried it as a ten year old each sheaf was as heavy as lead and full of thistles which scratched my tender arms until they bled.

The first corn was cut green so that it would ripen in the shock until ready for threshing. A well-made shock could stand any amount of wind but sometimes they would fall and lie drunkenly sideways and someone would have to go and prop them up again to stop the rain getting in. Armies of rooks and pigeons would descend on the bounty and cluster on top of the shocks. If left unchallenged they would eat the lot, so there was usually someone on hand to shoo them away, pretty well a full-time job in August.

There was great excitement when each field was nearing completion. Round and round went the binder, smaller and smaller became the square of standing corn. The rabbit population had been confined to that little patch and it grew smaller by the minute. Some more nervous than the rest would make a short dash out into the new and unfamiliar world of bare stubble, see the men with the sheaves, lose their nerve and scuttle back in again. When there were only two or three rounds left the tractor chugged to a halt and stood panting and chuckling, steam and oil leaking in equal amounts from its joints. The driver felt in his tool box and produced a long-handled hammer. The binder man had something like an elongated policeman's truncheon and the shock makers had pitchforks or sticks from the hedge.

This little army surrounded the corn and waded in whacking at the rabbits as they scurried round and between the tramping feet. There were shouts, 'Watch out with that bloody stick, boy; you near as dammit crippled me', 'Look up Jem, one a' comin' your way…' It was a poor field which did not produce half a dozen couple, each of which would be taken home and boiled with onions, carrots and an Oxo cube.

Best was when a field was cut all in the same day. Leave a half-cut field overnight and most of the rabbits would sneak out under cover of darkness. Some rabbits panicked and broke cover, striffing through the long stubble to the safety of the hedge. By some amazing coincidence the farmer and a couple of friends always seemed to be passing when a field was being finished and they stood round with their guns. Shots rang out and rabbits rolled over and over to lie still. It was not unknown in the excitement for the odd pellet to end up in a human gaiter and there was much hopping and cursing when this happened. The doctor was used to patients with pellet wounds at harvest time and one by one he picked them out to tinkle into his tin bowl. He seemed to take a malicious pleasure in dabbing on the iodine afterwards and seeing them jump.

The sport over, the driver returned to his seat, put his hammer in his box and hung his rabbit from the back of his tractor. The binder man had two and he tied them onto one of the long levers in front of him. The shockers put theirs in their lunch bags where they hung by the gate. A man with three might, if feeling generous, bestow one on someone who had none. All returned to their work, the field was finished and the team moved into the one next door.

When ripe some of the shocks were collected, stacked and thatched for threshing in the winter when there was plenty of time and not so much to do. The rest were threshed from the shock, ferried to the stackyard by a team of shock horses led by small boys of whom I was one, until the fields were all clear and ploughing could begin. The farming year was never-ending, always something to be done. Some threshing was not completed until after Christmas.

There came a time in early October when they celebrated the gathering of the corn with a Harvest Home or horkey. The success of the harvest was important to all in the village for overtime was earned, bills paid, machinery mended and new equipment bought, so all benefited. It was proper that thanks should be given. The horkey had roots in pagan times when the cruel and ancient goddess of farming was thanked and appeased by those on whom she had bestowed her benefits. The human sacrifice had gone long ago

but the straw dolly, which took the place of the victim, was still made and left in the church until spring when it was ploughed into the first furrow of the new season.

The horkey took place in the village hall. Trestle tables groaned under great pies, jars of pickles, loaves of crusty bread, slab-sided hams and sides of beef pink in the middle. Barrels of beer and cider stood in a rank along one wall. The folk came shuffling and tramping in, boots polished beetle black, the womenfolk in Sunday frocks and children on their best behaviour – for a while anyway. At first all were slightly nervous and restrained until beer loosened tongues and the talk grew louder. Folk sat on the folding chairs with plates piled high with meat, bread, pickled beetroot and sausages. The queue for the barrels was unending.

Then it was dancing to Frank Haddock, our gifted pianist. In later years a village band of mixed musicians and limited repertoire performed. The sweet, old-fashioned tunes led us into the valeta, the St Bernard's waltz, the Gay Gordons and other old favourites which were not too difficult. Even the children were dancing, while the men, clumsy and uncertain in their big boots, were steered firmly round the floor by their womenfolk for whom this was a rare night out and a chance not to be wasted.

There was a hammering on the table, silence fell and the squire rose to thank those who had worked so hard on the harvest, to compliment the old timers who had reached retirement and to comment on the quality of the crop. He was cheered mightily with much stamping of feet for he and his neighbours had paid for the feast. Then it was back to the dancing which grew more abandoned, the dust rising to a risky quickstep which often ended in human wreckage on a stack of folding chairs. A high spot was the hokey-cokey and one wondered how those floorboards could have taken such punishment as an army of folk with arms linked surged backwards and forwards.

The children grew tired and fractious, over-excited, overfull and, when their parents were not looking, they sipped more old ale than was good for them. Coats were pulled on, goodnights said and they tramped out into the night, up the High Street and down the lanes to their cottages. Overhead swung the great golden balloon which was the harvest moon, hovering over the stackyard elms. Somewhere an owl hooted and a dog barked. Then all was quiet. The old gods were appeased.

We were a Christian village and before long those black suits and best frocks were to have another airing, for harvest festival came next. It took a good week to decorate the church, a job for the village ladies organised by my mother with a sensitivity for precedence which would have defeated an international congress. The altar was decorated, reported in the parish magazine with quaint, olde worlde courtesy, by 'Mesdames Darby and Robinson'. Every lady had her own pitch and heaven help anyone who sought to intrude or offer gratuitous advice.

There was a carved wooden knob on the end of every pew. Each had a bunch of ears of wheat tied to it. The centrepiece of the altar was a huge loaf in the shape of a sheaf of corn, specially baked by Fred Cattell the village baker. There was a real sheaf on either side of it. The font vanished under a mountain of top-heavy, giant chrysanthemums, the altar was a fugue of cooking apples piled high in perilous pyramids. Flowers, scrubbed potatoes, vegetables from cottage gardens, giant marrows, leeks like billiard cues and a whole cornucopia of produce filled the place. The church was heady with the rich perfume of flowers, new bread and that distinctive aroma of Bramley apples. I smell it in my mind's nose as I write.

There was sometimes a problem with late gifts. Like unwanted babies, little parcels and baskets of vegetables would appear as late as Saturday night in the church porch. To avoid a diplomatic incident each had to be displayed, for the donor would arrive at the service and stare round eagerly to make sure that his contribution had been done justice.

For the service on Sunday the folk who had worked the land all summer came tramping in, their faces blackened with the sun and scrubbed shiny clean with soap. The men fidgeted with tight collars and twitched shoulders imprisoned inside jackets while their womenfolk, resplendent in dresses and sensible hats pinned on with spikes, nudged them in the ribs. The church was full, a faint odour of mothballs mingling with the scents of autumn.

The first hymn was announced, the organ struck up, there was a scraping of a hundred pairs of boots and shuffling of hymn books. Off we went with gusto. 'We plough the fields and scatter…' (long pause for breath) '…the good seed on the land…' Up into the great Norman arches and out through the holes in the stained glass and across the sunny fields with their lines of shocks floated the old anthem of thanks as it had done for hundreds of years.

My father, for thirty years the parson of this little community, delivered his address with its predictable theme of giving thanks for mercies from the Almighty. Some of the congregation reflected that it was all very well but The Almighty did not manage harvest all that well when He had it to himself. The service was punctuated by the trundling of apples dislodged by careless elbows, slipping from their shelves one by one and bouncing on a wooden pew. Time for another old faithful hymn, 'Come, ye thankful people, come: raise the song of harvest home. All is safely gathered in, ere the Winter storms begin…' We naughty boys in the choir would sing our own version of the second line. 'All is safely gathered in, Old John Hammence last agin…'

Then it was over and the folk dispersed, some of them reflecting gratefully that church-going was done with for another twelve months, barring a brief appearance at Christmas and Easter. The display in church was left and flowers removed as they wilted. The produce was divided into boxes and sent to all those in the village who were fallen on hard times to whom a little gift would be useful. Nothing was wasted, even the ears of corn on the pew ends being fed to father's chickens.

Harvest was over for another year and soon the wind blew chill and moaned in the chimney at night. We lay snug abed but perturbed by the ancient fear of mean old Winter lying in wait. We thought of things that must be done and speedily before he roared in with his icy breath.

Nowadays of course few people go to church; the harvest festival and the horkey have become dusty recollections in the memories of gaffers. The villages are inhabited by computer programmers who get their food pre-frozen, vacuum-packed, blow-dried and in tins from Sainsbury's and do not give thanks for it at all.

Coney Bill

Coney Bill was the rabbit catcher. He may have been only dimly aware of it, but his was an ancient craft. The Normans farmed rabbits which some said had been introduced by the Romans. They kept them in special towers jealously guarded against thieves and in those cold and hungry times fortunes were made from the sale of meat and fur. Almost a millennium later, Victorian farmers who struggled to farm marginal, sandy land, dug artificial warrens and bred wild rabbits for food and sport. The rabbit became the basis of a thriving rural industry and what was called the 'rabbit train' travelled weekly from Norfolk to London, its waggons hung with row upon row of coneys.

Landowners passed laws which they also enforced, meting out rough justice on a poor man who took a rabbit for the pot. It was hard for a hungry ploughman to resist the temptation of setting a snare by the hedge when he saw so much bounty running in front of his boots.

In time farming techniques improved and it became possible to grow barley on the thin land where once only rabbits could live and artificial warrens and rabbit trains became things of the past.

Other meat appeared in butchers' shops and the old Game Laws which protected rabbits were relaxed so that the bunny became sport and food for the poor man. Rabbits were good survivors and bred rapidly. This was just as well for they were bagged in the harvest field by men with sticks, shot as they dashed from a tussocky field, run down with lurchers, caught in long nets at night, ferreted, stalked with air rifles as they fed by the hedge and brought to the pot in a hundred ways which called for little financial expenditure but any amount of artfulness.

It was in the hungry 1930s that Coney Bill began to take notice. He had a natural understanding of rabbits and some said he thought like one. He even bore a passing resemblance to one, with his great hairy ears, buck teeth and stubble of beard which seemed to be never more and never less than seven days old. He swore he could hear the rabbits communicating underground: no one else claimed this knack but he assured all who would listen that it was so. When pressed about what sort of sound they made, he grew vague and slightly embarrassed. 'I dunno – they just sort of…talk.'

He was still at school when he joined the long netters. Quick on his feet, speedy to learn and able to keep his mouth shut, he was a natural. At first he was sent out to run back and forth in the stubble to start the rabbits dashing back home and into the waiting net. Usually this was done with a lurcher but 'the boys' were between dogs at the time. Sometimes in long stubble he would drag behind him a cocoa tin full of pebbles on a string. This rattled and rolled through the stalks so that every rabbit was started.

Then he graduated to net man, learning how to unroll it in the dark, insert the pegs and adjust the top lines with never a tangle. It was equally important to clear up well afterwards. A clean cut hazel stick overlooked and left sticking up in the turf would catch

a keeper's eye next morning and tell him as clearly as any words that he had been 'done'. Bill crouched waiting at one end of the net, his fingers gently touching the top cord. When a rabbit struck he was there, taking it out deftly and breaking its neck, throwing it to one side and waiting for the next one.

He could dispatch a rabbit in a second, throwing it across his knee, his wiry fingers feeling for neck muscles, a sharp cock of the wrist and a rabbit, one moment straining and tense, suddenly went limp. Not for him the amateur chopping with the edge of a hand as he had seen some of the gentry doing on the squire's shoot when he was beating. He was good at paunching, making a small nick with a knife sharp enough to shave with, holding front and back legs and giving a quick flick: the paunch flew out and the coney was ready for the dealer. He laughed to see some of the less experienced trying it, their hands a mess of blood and a ruined car-cass after.

There were run-ins with the keeper, of course, and once they had to abandon two good nets to avoid capture, but by then he had learned how to 'knit'. His lithe fingers flashed back and forth with a netting needle and in a week he had a new one made and in a fortnight they were back into full production. Their best night was one hundred and fourteen rabbits, a huge bag taken from the parkland behind the house of the squire himself. They could see lights click on and off in the bedroom windows as they worked. It took four of them two trips to carry that lot off the field plus all their gear. The squire had planned to shoot that warren on Boxing Day and there were hard words for the keeper when his posh guests came to find that the cupboard was bare.

In the 1950s rabbits were decimated by myxomatosis and Bill felt as though a part of him too had died. That fearful scourge had taken away something which had been important to him all his life and he wandered about like a man who had lost a limb. However, the rabbit is a survivor and it returned, in some places reaching the strength of the days before the plague. The long net was not appropriate now so, no longer a young man, Bill settled down to a life of ferreting which fitted in well with his seasonal work on farms and beating on shoots in the winter.

Several farmers had contracted him to thin out rabbits which were damaging the crops. Bill could easily get £1 for a clean, unshot rabbit, hard cash of which the tax man did not see a penny, and the farmer gave him a 'drink' for his help, so one way and another it was not a bad sort of life. Sometimes he bred from his famous ferrets and there was always a demand for their kittens.

You could find him most days in early spring crouching over a set of holes in a bank. His nets were carefully set and, an old hand, he never missed the secret bolthole under the tree root so easily overlooked by the less experienced. He did not smoke when working and kept quiet. The less the rabbits knew of his doings the better. He avoided tramping about over the holes especially when the frost made the ground iron-hard. The rabbits would not bolt well if they thought a human was waiting up above.

The nets set, he would slip in two or more of his ferrets, animals so tame that they gave the lie to the old myth about their natural ferocity. They would climb down his shirt and drape themselves round his net like a furry scarf. They had the run of his cottage, were as playful as kittens and would come to his call. He took a spade through force of habit but rarely did he need to dig, just chirrup between pursed lips and out they would come, their red-currant eyes blinking myopically in the sunlight.

Now he waited, an art at which he was a master. He stood close by on the downwind side of the holes, his back to a bush, not mov-ing until he seemed to be part of the scenery. His eyes were never still, watching the holes, listening intently for thumps under-ground which told him that rabbits were scuttling through their maze, fleeing the old enemy, until desperation drove them to make a dash for the open.

Then suddenly a rabbit would bolt, with a brown blur and a scuffle, the net would roll down the bank with a rabbit bundled up inside it, a grey and brown ball, fur sprouting through the meshes. Bill would pounce like a cat, a swift grab, a feel and a twist with those murderer's fingers and another pound's worth flung up on the grassy knoll. Quickly he reset the net and returned to his post.

Sometimes two or more rabbits would bolt at once but some-how Bill knew which one to grab first and for a few seconds his movements were swift as thought, rabbits dispatched, nets reset and back again to watch and wait. He never grew impatient and would wait all morning if need be. He trusted his ferrets and knew they were busy down below. When he felt that time was up he would crouch at the hole and chirrup and out they would come, one at a time, looking for a titbit.

He packed up, taking up the nets, untangling them, picking out twigs and rolling each one up neatly to be ready for next time. Old habit made him tidy up, leaving no trace of his passing. There was no longer the need for secrecy but his ingrained caution held good; no point in letting all and sundry know your business and where you had been. In this way he worked his way down a hedge and along the bottom and he might end up with a dozen and a half rabbits on a good morning.

Each one legged and paunched, hanging neatly from the spade handle, the ferret box and net bag on the other shoulder, he made his way slowly home to his cottage in the lower lane. The rabbits he hung in his outhouse to cool and at the end of the week the man would come in his van and take them away.

He sat in a battered chair by a fire of apple logs and reflected that what little he had he owed to the rabbits. For over sixty years they had kept food in his belly, shag tobacco in his pipe and a shilling in his pocket. Although he killed them without a thought, he loved them and depended on them, seeing them as a harvest put on this earth by the Almighty to help the poor man.

His was a philosophy that American Indian, Eskimo, Zulu and Aborigine would have understood perfectly.

Country Bike

In the *real* country we did not go in for this nonsense of flashy bikes. Nobody in their right mind would be seen dead on some tortured piece of high tensile, tubular metal with drop handlebars, a saddle which cleaves your bottom like a scimitar and narrow tyres which seek and find every rut and pothole in the road. Such a toy was more for callow youths interested in cutting a dash with the girls than for a sober citizen travelling safely from point A to point B. The serious cyclist eschewed such ostentation as undependable, ephemeral and uncomfortable.

As for the latest craze for mountain bikes, some of which could set you back £1000, the mind boggled and one could but gawp at precocious youngsters flashing round dangerously on the pavements, leaping over obstacles and clad from head to toe in body armour to protect their limbs against the spills which seem to be an integral part of that sport. Such abuse of two wheels was a million miles removed from the simple need to transport a human cargo from here to there and back.

A villager's bike was a sturdy affair painted black. It took a good man to lift it bodily from the ground for it was solid, dependable, made to last and designed to serve at least three generations of cyclists with minimum maintenance. The handlebars stood upright and four square, the chrome coming off in flakes although no-one minded as such a trifle was purely cosmetic and did not affect performance. There were stout rubber grips which sat easily in the clenched hand, although often one of them was missing. On the older models a metal step protruded from the axle of the back wheel to aid mounting, a nod in the direction of the penny-farthing from which all cycles were descended.

Ladies' models were enhanced by what was known as a skirt guard. Women cycled in long, heavy skirts, for the lycra body stocking would not have done at all, even if it had been invented. A stout cord was laced back and forth like a spider's web from rear mudguard to axle which prevented flowing clothing from being muddied or entangled in the back wheel.

The three-speed gear was considered a bit showy but one or two of the under-fifties liked them. A lever bolted on to the crossbar worked a metal cable which allowed you to change down when going up one of the two hills in the village, shifting smoothly with a quick back pedal and adjustment of the lever, back to full power when safely on the flat. Sturmey Archer made the standard three-speed, a name like Aston Martin to roll round the mouth and savour for it was redolent of high technology and sophisticated machinery.

Lights were not often required, for cycling was mainly a daylight activity. The carbide lamp was just about obsolete so now expensive machines had a dynamo, a thing like a plump little bottle screwed on by the back mudguard. To activate it you twisted it round until a serrated wheel on top of it pressed against the side of the tyre. As you pedalled this generated the electricity to work your lights.

Rarely did one work for more than a month for they were prone to failure. Battery-operated lights could be bought for front and rear. To light up you screwed down a knob on the top until the terminals touched, a circuit was created and you were away. I never knew of a set which worked for more than two expeditions for the screwing mechanism suffered from design faults – the rain penetrated the top and spoiled the battery and even when working it did no more than illuminate a little pool of tarmac a yard in front of your wheel. When your lamp holder was bent, as it usually was, you were less lucky and it shone bravely up into the night sky, glinting on the underside of the bushes: or else it glared down with full power onto the top of your front wheel.

In the end most nocturnal cyclists took their chance, relying on the fact that there were only three cars in the village to knock them down. They knew every bump in the roads and the village policeman was sure to be safely at home or in the pub. In case of trouble it was easy to nip off and wait by the hedge until whatever it was had passed.

Another vital accessory was the basket. This was made of wicker and strapped onto the front handlebars. Often it had sagged through age and the carrying of heavy groceries, bags of mushrooms, small dogs, dead rabbits and other useful payload. I have written elsewhere of the station master whose basket was a wooden box for taking home coal from the heap at the station.

You might have a supplementary basket behind the seat in place of the saddle-bag, a largely wasted reticule given over to the puncture repair outfit, a multi-socket spanner and a rolled yellow cape in case of rain. Sometimes a small satchel of hide leather with a patent metal fastener took its place. Others had a metal, slatted rack fixed above the rear wheel onto which bulky items of luggage might be tied with binder string. The man who worked a small market garden made a trailer which fastened to his saddle post. In this he transported his tools and watering can and once I saw him toiling along head wind, towing a sack of potatoes.

Women carried small children on a little saddle fixed to the front. The child's legs hung down on either side of the wheel and while it would have given a modern Health and Safety gauleiter a fit, many children travelled hundreds of miles in safety in this way before they became cyclists in their own right.

An accessory not available as standard from Messrs Raleigh or Hercules was essential for the many shooters in the village. Onto the saddle post you fixed a large wire hook and from the handlebars you hung a leather strap. A shotgun fitted perfectly into this, lying along the crossbar so as not to impede pedalling, the barrels supported by the strap and the grip of the gun lying snug in the hook which you had padded with a little insulating tape.

Guns travelled thousands of miles in this way as did fishing rods.

One mishap occurred when a fisherman was free-wheeling down Bury Lane, one of our hills which led down to the Fen. This was a chance to get up serious speed although toiling back up it was another matter. The angler had a short spinning rod made up and lying in his hook and strap carrier. Somehow the tip of the rod got into the front spokes. The machine stopped dead and the rider flew in a graceful parabola to land on the road on his ear. Youth and elasticity were on his side and while he was badly grazed, no bones were broken.

Cycling was done sedately with no sense of rush, apart from forays down Bury Lane. The idea was to arrive safe and composed and not flustered and muddy. Older cyclists travelled so slowly that they could be overhauled by a lively pedestrian while they wobbled along seeming to defy gravity. Burton Darby rode with a metal pail hanging from each handlebar. Even his was a ground-eating pace and given time, of which there was no shortage, there was nowhere denied you – you got there in the end. Your basket loaded with provisions and the safe solidity of a stout saddle and the bicycle beneath you, gave you a sense of confidence and security, and if it was head wind on the way there, you had the comfort of knowing it would be behind you on the way back.

Once it was a universal form of transport in an unmotorised age. Environmentally friendly, cheap, reliable, good exercise and proof against any weather apart from deep snow, the bike was the thread which bound communities together. Now there are two cars outside every house and cycling has become the province of small boys, Olympic athletes and health freaks.

As for the old bikes, they never wore out for they were made to last. In forgotten sheds among colonies of spiders, robins' nests and dust they lean abandoned but still proud, skirt guards, leather saddles hard as iron, parcel racks, three-speeds, flat tyres and faulty dynamos all in place, defying the years. If inanimate objects may be said to dream, their dreams might be that when fossil fuels finally run out their day will return.

Blind Bob's

It closed some time ago, a clutch of ghastly neo-Georgian executive residences (one dare not call them houses) where it used to stand. A pub is an essential part of a community like the school, church and shop. Today there are too many joyless dormitories lacking more than one of them. Such villages are sad places. The pub is not a place where a man goes to get drunk, although as the Irish say, there is 'drink taken'. If a village boasts six pubs it does not follow that he will stagger from one to another and consume six drinks. One will suit his taste in beer, landlord, company and general ambience and there he goes for bonhomie, the company of like-minded souls and the opportunity to put the wide world to rights in a way which he might find difficult at home. Wives may grind their teeth, but that's the way it is.

Blind Bob and his wife Vera ran The Royal Oak down at the end of the village. The decor was nothing spectacular, 1930s 'grot' really, but as Bob was blind there was no reason to waste good money on something he could not see and from which only others would benefit. Once he was heard to mutter something about 'redecorating'. Instant consternation all round, and to a man the locals insisted he left things as they were; they preferred it like that and anyway, posh pubs were two a penny.

Having a blind landlord was unusual, one might say unique in the licensed trade. Bob kept his beer in great casks on racks at floor level behind the bar. He fussed round them like a shepherd with a flock of fat, brown sheep. To serve a pint he needed to take a glass from the shelf, stoop to a barrel, fill the glass to the brim, transfer it safely to the bar, take the money and hand over the change. Not in half a lifetime did I see him get it wrong save once. He was dispensing whisky from an empty bottle, the roar of conversation in the bar preventing him from hearing the trickling of the precious fluid.

Bob could fill a pint mug by listening to the sound of the ale and not, as enemies alleged, by keeping his thumb inside the rim. The brimming glass would be placed on the counter so full that I have seen a sighted customer spill a few precious drops as he conveyed it to his lips. Hand him a note of the realm be it a tenner or a twenty and Bob would always enquire, 'A fiver?' as he felt it. He knew full well exactly what it was and just once in five hundred times the punter, his mind on other matters, would reply, 'That's right'.

That bar was Bob's world and he knew to the inch where everything was. His sensitive fingers brushed lightly on the edge of the till or the bottle opener fixed on the bar, landmarks in his dark world, and he knew exactly where he stood. He knew that the fourth bottle from the end was scotch, fifth gin and so on, his fingers running delicately along the row until he came to the right one. Mental arithmetic was his forte and he could calculate the cost of the most complicated round of drinks in a second, feel in the till and hand over the right change.

His affliction could be turned to advantage. As a matter of courtesy to his customers he was reluctant to call time, even in the later days of enlightened licensing laws and one night a passing police car stopped outside. The officers were 'furriners', unfamiliar with the pub and its unusual landlord and they strode in. 'Don't you know it's almost midnight?' they demanded angrily. Bob was thunderstruck. 'Well, bless my soul', he said, 'and they told me it was only quarter past ten'.

Once a lad came from town to empty the money from the cigarette machine. He sat counting a pile of coins on the table when he felt a need to visit the toilet. How could he leave his heap of cash unattended with a clutch of local reprobates standing round? 'Don't worry', said Bob, 'I'll watch it for you'. Gratefully the stranger hurried out, leaving his takings under the watchful gaze of the only blind landlord in the kingdom.

Bob was an avid radio listener, horse-racing expert and jazz fanatic. He could tell you what horse won what race in any year, the name of jockey and owner and as often as not, how much he had won on it or lost by betting on some slower nag. He knew who played second saxophone in Duke Ellington's band of 1936 and the history of most people in the county unto the third and fourth generation.

His fund of knowledge on a wide range of subjects was inexhaustible. Not only did he listen carefully but he was blessed with a retentive memory. Many a discussion was settled by his encyclopaedic knowledge; 'We'll let Bob settle it', they would say. Let the pub door open and a footfall tramp three times on the lino and before the visitor spoke Bob would know who had come in, where they had been, where they would be going after they left and what they were about to order to drink.

This bizarre and unusual establishment attracted a congregation of customers who were themselves a mixture of the eccentric, the flamboyant, the unclubbable and the diverse. Poachers rubbed shoulders with gamekeepers, senior policemen in spotted neckerchiefs talked to itinerant musicians, university dons in corduroys chatted to eighty-year-old farm labourers in suits who had ploughed with horses. Each had his tale to tell, his philosophy of life, his little gem of personal wisdom, for the crowd in the bar of The Oak was classless and cosmopolitan.

This is not to say that debate could not be stern verging on the acrimonious. I have seen men grow hot under their grimy collars arguing about frogs, the whole pub drawn into the discussion, each man with his passionate point of view. Folk jabbed one another in the chest, shouting, 'And I tell you... my old dad allus reckoned that a female frog ...' Faces reddened and voices rose until someone defused the conflict with a fatuous observation and the debate dissolved in gales of laughter. At other times it might be how to grow cauliflowers or the quickest way to skin a rabbit, with a demonstration on the spot to prove the point.

In summer, on the pub mantelpiece next to last year's faded calendar, accumulated a strange harvest festival of misshapen vegetables. Many of the locals were gardeners and a grotesque row of double parsnips, carrots in amusing and suggestive shapes, short, fat leeks next to thin, long ones and knobbly potatoes stood as caricatures of themselves and those who had grown them.

It was a place of music, not the dreadful canned variety from juke box or wall-mounted speakers but the real thing. Often on a Sunday lunch-time a folk band would set up in the corner, the sweet squealing of an old fiddle and a wheezing accordion singing of times past. Any musician in the throng was welcome to join in and many did. Other times a country-and-western band, led by the incomparable Pete Sayers who had played at the Grand Old Opry in Memphis, Tennessee, would turn up for an impromptu concert. Vera would produce a huge tray of sausage rolls while the banjos danced, guitars thrummed and violin played long into the night. Often it was a jazz band, three or four musicians happening to find themselves in the bar at once, each having his instrument in the car: two pints of Bob's real ale was all it took to get them going.

One foggy night two strangers dropped in having lost their way. It was a pea-souper and they had stopped to ask directions at the first pub they found. They must have been well out of their way to have stumbled down that little lane which led nowhere much. They sat in the corner sipping a drink when a trio of the finest jazz musicians in East Anglia struck up. The strangers gawped to find such a pearl in so rough an oyster and stayed a whole evening before departing. One could imagine them recounting their experiences later if and when they got home and also, perhaps, setting out again trying to rediscover this amazing place, failing to do so and then wondering if it had all been a dream.

We celebrated Burns' night with haggis all round. Ranuld the cabinet maker and master piper donned full Highland regalia for the occasion. The sound of his apparatus was well nigh deafening in that small space. He recited Burns' ode 'To a Haggis' with authentic fervour and many extravagant gestures and, at the critical moment, plunged his dirk into the creature.

On a Saturday evening shooting parties would come in tired and wet after a day on the windy fen. They sat round the fire in their boots and breeks discussing the day as Labradors and spaniels steamed quietly on the mat. Once a group of punks dropped in; they smiled at our Edwardian shooting clobber and we shooters chuckled at the safety-pins in noses, shaven heads, holey jeans and tie-dyed T-shirts. All was good natured but it showed our rich diversity as a people.

Once on the way home from shooting I passed a rat run over in the road. It was a monster, a Goliath among rats so I stopped and picked it up. In The Oak I brought the talk round to the weights of various creatures. My rat was produced and all present hefted it and made a calculated guess. In the end we ran a book on it putting a pound each in the kitty. Vera was called to adjudicate and she came from the back with her kitchen scales on which she weighed her flour, to pronounce her judgement of Solomon. Winner took all, but it was the butcher who got it right, a man used to judging weights, although some wag felt that he would have added the weight of his thumb, his daily custom in his shop.

The rat alone would not do; we were getting the taste for weighing things. Someone else had a monstrous pheasant in their car boot, another a hefty partridge, a third a jumbo rabbit, each to be solemnly passed from hand to hand and so the evening wore away while the rain drummed on the casement. Those outside the group were invited to join in the game, even a courting couple in the corner although the young lady did not care to touch any dead creature unless it had first been swathed in a polythene bag. Many pounds changed hands that night.

Some Thursdays we received a visit from a minibus full of patients from a home for the mentally handicapped. They were harmless and often delightful people although their behaviour was unconventional. They had a minder with them and, typically, The Oak was the one of the few places where they were made welcome. They spent happy evenings there, one strumming an imaginary guitar, another talking to himself, a third stroking the cranium of anyone with a bald head, his friend drumming rhythmically on the bar. We were used to them and made them feel at home. One night they happened to be there when no local was present. Two London CID men passing through dropped in for a pint and found the place full of folk behaving oddly. As they left one of them took Bob by the sleeve and whispered, 'Who are these people?' Bob solemnly informed him that they were only a few of the locals out for a quiet evening.

To those who loved it The Oak was something special in their lives. It was the hub of a community, a strange and disparate brotherhood, a pub for men, unashamedly chauvinist but it was the lynchpin which held us all together, always welcoming, always someone interesting to talk to and a place to take visitors you wanted to impress with the fact that such a place existed.

In the end the brewery closed it down and sold the site. The cold hand of the accountants, who judge all human life by the bottom line on a balance sheet, fell upon it and they decided that it would be more profitable sold off, along with Bob's orchard and car park. Petitions were signed, angry and tearful letters written but the faceless ones were adamant.

The last day drew close, then it was here and we had a proper funeral, with a coffin paraded down the high street, Ranuld playing a sad pibroch on his pipes and a New Orleans marching band to give The Oak a proper send off. It was a night to remember, a party which ran on into the small hours, for no policeman now could take away Bob's licence. Not a drop of alcohol remained in the place at the end of it. Next morning the building was shuttered, cold and empty, the fun, the laughter and the roar of conversation which had been part of it for three centuries was for ever silenced.

That strange company of regulars dispersed, many of them seeing each other no more, for The Oak was all they had in common. Others sought out other, lesser pubs and did their best to settle down but all felt an ache that a vital part of their lives had been taken from them.

Sometimes I go and stand on the pavement gazing at the place where it was. I hear a ghostly echo of music, friendly voices discussing gardening, cricket and eels and the door handle which always squeaked, telling Bob that he had a customer. Sometimes, when it is especially quiet and I am in receptive mood I swear I hear the voice of Bob himself, intoning one of his oft repeated one-liners, 'I'll buy you a drink when I see you next'.

The labels on the bottles read: SLOE GIN 1794, CARROT WINE 1911, BEETROOT WINE 1911

Mellow Fruitfulness

Autumn in the village was a busy time for humans and animals alike. Living closer to Nature than modern man, people were more sensitive to the frisson which told that winter was on its way. I speak of days when a farm worker earned less than a fiver a week, there were no cut-price supermarkets and the village shop stocked only basic commodities. To survive it was vital that supplies were laid in to see a family through the hungry days until spring returned. In hard winters the weak went to the wall, sickly children and frail old-timers were likely to die unless, by systematic gathering and hoarding in autumn, a good store of provisions was put by.

The animals and birds felt it too. Before the wind swung round to the north and east they sensed impending change. Mist hung heavy in the mornings, rooks wheeled high in the sky cawing wildly, the grey squirrels scampered, gathering walnuts and acorns, burying them and later forgetting where they were hidden. Woodpigeons flew out in great flocks to raid the drilled corn fields, the first of the wild swans and wigeon arrived on the marsh, driven south by the frost in their breeding grounds on the northern tundra. Mallard filled the evening skies like clouds of smoke as they flighted out across a blood-red sunset to feed on distant stubbles. The scent of garden bonfires perfumed the air.

Every cottage kitchen was a buzz of activity. Great vats of boiling jam with their satellite wasps stood on the cooker. Jars of pickles marched in rows in the larder like platoons of dumpy soldiers. Each had its little mob-cap of a cover tied down with waxed string and a label stating the contents and the date. Stone jars were filled with water-glass in which eggs were preserved. In those pre-battery days eggs were in short supply in winter when hens went off the lay and it was important to save as many as possible.

In the dry cool of the loft were rows of apples. Some varieties such as Cox's and Bramleys were well known as 'keepers' and each was carefully checked for bruises and blemishes before being wrapped in newspaper and laid in rows, none touching another, safe from frost, waiting for the moment they would be needed.

In the garden stood a mighty clamp of potatoes. All the spuds were dug, the main crop, King Edwards, being popular then, and heaped in a pyramid. The mound was covered with straw and over that a thick layer of earth with a small gap at the top for ventilation. Potatoes kept like this would survive the hardest frost and the deepest snow. If all else failed, a family with a good potato clamp would never go hungry.

Carrots and parsnips were stored in sand which kept them better than earth and prevented them sprouting from their tops. A pit in the garden still full of sand from last year would be excavated afresh, filled with the precious vegetables and covered over. Still growing in the garden were winter cauliflowers, cabbages and the old favourite Brussels sprouts which could stand the cold. Onions were tied in strings and hung out in the shed. The old knack of tying in their tops so that they locked together was a trick known to every cottage gardener.

The gardener saw to it that he saved enough seed for next year's sowing. No point in paying nursery prices when you could strip the dry pods of runner beans and broad beans, allow a couple of leeks to go to seed, hold back a few small potatoes and save a jam-jar full of dwarf bean seeds. They were kept dry and away from mice in the shed and saved quite a few shillings next spring.

As well as chickens, many households kept a pig in a sty at the end of the garden. In the war you were allocated a meal ration sufficient for one pig, provided it was supplemented with cabbage leaves and kitchen waste. A pig is a wonderful converter of rubbish

into sides of bacon as well as being a charming and intelligent creature. It was said that pigs could see the wind and on a more practical level you could eat every bit of it except the squeak.

We had two pigs named Boswell and Johnson. They were always getting out and with their iron snouts rootling about in the churchyard, having to be herded home from around the gravestones. Once father had a whispered message in the middle of Holy Communion that 'the pigs are out'. He rushed out from church, his vestments flowing in the wind, backed by the male members of the congregation, and a fine sight they made dodging round 'RIP' and 'Dearly Beloved' like rugby players as they rounded up the fugitives.

Boswell and Johnson would stand at the gate of their sty begging to be scratched. Taking a stick I would scrape behind their ears while they closed their eyes in ecstasy, gave little squeaks and grunts of satisfaction and leaned against the wall, quite overcome. I would fetch them an old cabbage stalk and watch with delight as they munched it up. There was no room in the old countryside for sentimentality, especially with winter coming on and while I felt a pang of sorrow, it was strangely exciting when their nemesis arrived in the form of Joe Linford and his boy in their rubber aprons, come to do the dirty deed.

It was a personal grievance that I was forbidden to watch but nevertheless poor old Boswell and Johnson were strung up, their throats slit, their bodies flung into burning straw to remove their whiskers and cut up into bits. Two days after, they came back from Joe's in great tubs of brine neatly jointed, all the innards in a separate bucket. The blood made black pudding. The hams were smoked and hung from the scullery ceiling, bacon salted and the head and trotters made into pork cheese sometimes known as brawn. With herbs and spices, salt and seasoning it was a lovely jelly tapped out from the pudding basin to be cut in slices and eaten with brown bread. It had little black streaks in it caused, said mischievous old grannies, by an eyeball left in, 'to see you through the week'.

Next spring father would do a deal with the farmer down the lane and two new, miniature Boswell and Johnsons arrived.

Another important autumn job was wood chopping. The chain-saw was not available so it was the crosscut with me on one end and my father on the other all the livelong day. Then it was the axe, not a proper splitting axe with wide shoulders but a felling axe, quite wrong for the job for it bound in and took an age to extricate. Many good trees had blown down in the gale of 1947 so there was no shortage of wood. Most of it was elm which is not good for burning being sullen and slow. It is also tough and knotty, hard to saw and even harder to split but at least it was free.

Bit by bit we amassed a goodly pile of logs which were stacked by the outhouse. They dried better if gaps were left between and we would build up a neat wall of them, one row this way the other that, until it was too high for me to put another on top. A family with a pile of logs, a full coal-shed and 5 gallons of paraffin in a tin drum could afford to think with some complacency of the coming winter.

We had a walnut tree and the nuts came pattering down onto the carpet of dead leaves. These were carefully gathered, scrubbed and stored in a barrel of sand in which they would keep indefinitely. A gale would cast down walnuts still unripe in their green, outer casings. These were put in jars of vinegar and became pickled walnuts.

As well as the serious harvest from the garden there was a secondary bounty from the fields and hedges. We pricked purple-stained fingers gathering blackberries for jam and mixing with the blemished cooking apples to make one of the countryman's favourite puddings, blackberry and apple pie. Hips and haws could be collected and made into jellies with a hot, peppery flavour. Bullaces and sloes dotted the hedges as did elderberries with heavy black clusters of fruit. These were good for wine making and many a village goodwife could make wine which made your hair stand on end. Harmless enough it looked in the glass and it even tasted innocuous but after a couple of slugs you went wobbly in the legs.

Wine could be made from any vegetable matter and adventurous spirits experimented with wheat, potato peelings, rhubarb and even carrots. There was little flavour to suggest the source material but it was all potent stuff which would have done for moon

rocket fuel. It was better kept for a year or two to mature so each autumn you made a fresh batch and drank that of three years before. The top shelf of the pantry held a row of demijohns each bubbling, the liquid in turmoil, giving off a yeasty smell. In time it settled down and cleared, was poured into old bottles, corked, labelled and racked in the cellar where people used to come and wait out the air raids.

We shared the wild harvest of the hedgerows with the field mice, birds and squirrels, gathering baskets of cobnuts, sweet chestnuts and the tiny beech mast with its nubby white kernels, good for just a nibble and then gone. It was an instinct, a primitive urge to fatten up on this last opportunity before the frost and snow locked away the food for months. We felt it as strongly as did the animals and birds.

An important wild crop in autumn was mushrooms. These grew down on the stubbles and meadows of the fen. They were not universal and you had to know where to go, a secret which no bribe or torture could extricate from a mushroom man. You set out early in the morning so no-one could see where you went, strolling through the dewy stalks seeking the little eruptions in the soil where a new mushroom was forcing its way up. Those already well up and going brown round the edges could be all right after the first frost, but often you removed the stipe and found them riddled with tiny holes, caused by the dreaded fly which made them inedible.

A warm, damp autumn would produce great swathes of them and a picker could gather a basketful of mushrooms the size of dinner plates without walking more than a dozen paces. They were not easy to preserve although mushroom ketchup could be made. Some old folk threaded them on strings to dry in the sun. When soaked in water they resumed their old shape if not quite their old flavour.

We were not experts on fungi but some of the older folk knew and picked varieties other than the common field or horse mushrooms which were easily identified and safe. To pick fungi of which you were less than a hundred per cent certain was madness.

It was a short harvest but for a month we ate mushrooms fried, in stews, raw, roasted with the meat and in every imaginable way. Their flavour was rich and pungent, far better than modern, cultivated mushrooms.

We let little go to waste for, with ingenuity, a use could be found for everything. There was a philosophy in those hard times which ran, 'Use it up; make it last; wear it out', while 'waste not want not' was our way of life. Even the green tomatoes in the garden which would never ripen were made into chutney rather than thrown away. What little vegetable waste was left after the pigs had done with it was composted and dug into the garden. Very rarely was anything thrown into the dustbin for almost everything could be recycled, even ashes from the fire.

When winter came the meat ration could be supplemented by the sportsmen. Almost everyone in the village had a rusty gun and a fishing rod. Pike, eels and perch, shoaled in the rivers, and all were delicious. Rabbits lay out in the rough grass, there for the taking by a man with ferret, net or gun and the wildfowl swarmed down on the marshes. Some farmers gave permission for partridge shooting on their wide acres and a brace and a half of the little brown birds made a welcome feast. For Christmas most homes had a cockerel or two scratching in the hen run or a couple of geese kept specially. A turkey was a luxury and who would wish to buy such a thing when a fat goose strutted in the yard?

Few writers captured the countryman's unease at the coming of winter better than Dorothy Hartley: '...the harvest folk have been and gone home again and the barns are full and Autumn is come... Then one night it turns cold and we lie closer for warmth and stay waking a little, thinking of the things we must do – speedily, for it is winter'.

Things were not nearly so easy for the poor folk who lived in towns far from the green acres, but, by the time November arrived, the cottager with his load of logs, smoked hams, pickles, eggs, vegetables in clamps, apples in the loft and home-made wine in the cellar was entitled to sleep easy, with a smile on his face.

Winter

With a skirl and a clamour the first migrating wildfowl swing down from leaden skies and with a swish of paddles land on the flooded water meadow. The mean wind has pellets of snow on its breath, and it lies steady as a constellation in the cruel quarters of north and east.

The country calendar does not cease and the farm boys are ploughing, the hiss of steel plough shares slicing the stubbles and the cloud of gulls like scraps of paper following behind. Work goes on, but at home the fire of apple logs smells sweet while the scent of rabbit pie and dumplings gives assurance that tonight at least all will be well.

Smoke from the smithy chimney drifts and the hammer rings. The shooter is out to ambush duck on the marsh, or hunt down the wily pheasant in the rushes. At night that rascal the local poacher is out under the moonlit trees engaged in the ancient running battle of wits between himself and his arch enemy, the keeper.

A family with a good store of logs, vegetables, smoked bacon, a shotgun and a fishing rod will see the winter safely out until the first house martin renews nature's ancient promise of better times.

Hedging Bets

The American poet Robert Frost had a point when he observed, 'Something there is that does not love a wall', but his view might have been different about a hedge. Our green and pleasant land is seamed with hedges, their total mileage more than that of motorways and they are to be treasured as valuable enhancers of the countryside. The most ancient ones ought to be regarded as national monuments for they are as old as the churches.

The earliest were set by the Norman conquerors to keep the common folk away from their new manor houses. Traffic the other way was encouraged, for the hedge had a deer leap cut in it so that the lord's hares and deer could jump across and feed in the vegetable patches and sparse crops of the villeins and as easily return. Where such an ancient hedge may be found it will be loaded in autumn with crab apples, sloes and the red-hot berries of hawthorn.

Most of our hedges were established in the eighteenth and nineteenth centuries during the Enclosures. They marked field boundaries, reduced erosion of the topsoil, sheltered byres from the north wind and intitiated early attempts at crop rotation. The fields were small, for there was only so much one man and a horse could accomplish in a day. It was only when the giant machinery of the modern age came to the farms that small fields were found to be limiting and wasteful of land.

The old rule of thumb for ageing a hedge was to count the number of species of plant in it – one for every ten years was about right, so a hedge containing ten different trees would be a century old. The system breaks down with really old hedges.

A good old hedge is a benefit in other ways. Birds love to nest there. Dense woodland is not suitable for many wild creatures which prefer the edges where there is light, air and space: birds are creatures of the boundaries. A good hedge holds food, protection from sparrowhawks and magpies and many nesting territories in a limited span. Fox hunters can leap a hedge if it is well managed and cut to the right height. Poor folk turn out in autumn and gather the fruits which they preserve to help them through the winter. Little do they think that they have the French invader of a thousand years ago to thank for their brimming baskets. Fieldmice, foxes, badgers, rabbits, stoats and weasels also know that a good hedge is a happy hunting ground and a safe place to live.

On the old partridge manors quickset hedges were allowed to grow tall. To shoot driven grey partridges over a high, unkempt hedge is one of the great icons of the sport of field shooting. A covey would fly forward, cross the hedge, see the waiting guns beyond and burst like a star-shell to all points, banking and flaring, making this the cream of game-bird shooting in the days of our forefathers. Farms not blessed with covies of the little brown birds had to maintain their hedges properly.

Before the days of mechanisation tending the hedges was a major winter task when there was little else for farm workers to do. When the autumn ploughing was finished it was all hands to hedging, which they did in rotation. By the time they had worked the whole farm it would be time to start again. A neglected hedge grew sparse and straggly. Trees shot up in it and between them thin places developed so that the wind whistled cold between. A lazy man might force his way through rather than go the long way round, and after that a bullock would squeeze through, so the hedge lost nine-tenths of its usefulness.

The art of hedge laying is a dying one. Time was when every farm labourer could do it, chopping and bending his 22 yards a day – a chain, that ancient measurement from which the length of a cricket pitch is derived. A man would stand contemplating his span for the day as he filled his pipe. He could tell in a few moments which saplings needed cutting out and which he would redirect to bind in a thin place. It took him the rest of the day to execute it. The key saplings would be nicked and bent down, leaving the sap-carrying core intact. This would be woven in or pegged with a stake so that new growth in spring would shoot up and intertwine with the existing to make a dense frieze.

His tools, the slasher or billhook, stout leather mittens, beetle and stakes, were as old as the Normans themselves and doubtless the technique of laying changed little. Each district had its unique design of billhook. It was only after two springs had passed that a man could see just how well or badly he had done his job. A well-laid hedge would have the new growth mingling with the old creating a dense, protective screen. He could stand downwind of it on a cold day and feel, as he might say, 'a coat warmer', for the wind would be fragmented and its sting reduced by the tightly woven mesh of thorn, crab and field maple.

The hedging gang would take their mid-morning 'dockey' break of cold tea from a screw-topped bottle and a hunk of bread and fat bacon or cheese. As they ate they eyed their 'stitch' of work and that of their neighbours making secret comparisons, noting a wandering briar which, for aesthetic reasons only, needed trimming back as soon as the break was over. The boy was on hand to rake and burn the brash which they left in a prickly row along the headland. He was armed with a pitchfork and a box of matches and woe betide him if his fire blew smoke into the faces of the workers.

Their day's work done, their chain of hedge laid, they put on their jackets, shouldered tools and tramped off back to the farmyard where their bicycles leaned safe in the cart shed. Behind them in the gathering gloom a row of red pin-pricks of dying fires showed where they had been.

Today much has changed. The mechanisation of farms, the decimation of the army of land workers and lack of time have created between them a system of instant hedge management. A gap in a hedge which, through neglect, was no longer stock-proof might be filled with a strand of barbed wire, that hideous stuff which is the curse of the countryside. How many horses have gone down because of it, how many dogs been lacerated, how many wellingtons punctured and how many pairs of corduroy breeches rent asunder it would be hard to guess but it must be thousands.

The modern method of hedge maintenance is a flail mounted on a tractor. This machine roars along a hedge smashing rather than cutting all outstanding growth from flimsy twigs to stout branches. The residue is pulverised and spewed out in a mash of prickles and shoots which are the curse of passing cyclists for they cause many punctures. The result looks neat enough and one man can do in a day what it would have taken the old gang a month to complete but time now is money.

The modern hedge lacks the beauty of a laid one. Its outside is too dense to allow easy access for birds to nest and the hedge fruits tend to grow best on older more neglected growth. For all that the hedge is still an asset in the landscape, a haven for many plants, animals and birds. Many hundreds of miles were ripped out in the 1960s when a philistine government offered financial incentives for such vandalism.

Thankfully the trend has been reversed. The small fields which were right for the days after the agricultural revolution were inappropriate for combine harvesters and drills with 20-foot spans, but farmers overdid it and many fields were made too large. Look at the wheat plains of the West Country or parts of East Anglia to see the full horror of a hedgeless countryside and how soulless it has become.

Hedges are being replanted. There are still many miles fewer than there were a century ago but at last officialdom is making a move in the right direction. An English countryside without a hedge to break the monotony and provide shelter for birds, not to mention the main ingredient of elderberry wine and satisfaction for the eye, is indeed a poor and barren place.

Wild Goose Chase

Grey geese do strange things to wildfowlers. Their myriad armies, wild skirling, the romance of their great saga from Iceland and their wariness make them something worth hunting. Their magic draws the lone fowler back to the saltings year after year until old age prevents his coming more. Lying on the sick bed of his infirmity still he can hear in his head that wild chorus, see the echelons of the skeins printed across moonlit clouds in a wild Scottish sky.

An obsessed and lonely goose shooter who had a bad case of goose fever swam into my ken long ago in my student days. I met him tramping slowly off the Solway marshes one bitter January morning. Like me he was a winter migrant, a once-a-year goose

chaser who lost a week of his life in that northern Valhalla of wildfowling. We both loved the lure of those great birds, the scent of the saltings and the bulk of the snow-capped, extinct volcano which men call Griffel.

His name was George and he was an assistant bank manager, his gold-rimmed 'readers' and receding hair the stereotypes of his profession. He had been inspired by shooting writers who described wild mornings and thrilling flights, and in the family Morris he slogged up from the Midlands. He stayed in a guest house and passed every morning and evening and sometimes the daytime too waiting on the marsh, patient as an old heron, for just a chance at one of the grey birds.

His income was fixed, but 'costly his habit as his purse could buy', his fowling kit bought with care – a waxproof smock, rubber waders, scarf, gloves and woolly hat. On lanyards round his neck hung the obligatory binoculars, whistle and goose call and he was armed with a Magnum shotgun made by that fine old Norwich firm, Rosson.

George chose the first week of the New Year for his holiday, easier to get away then and keep the peace at home and not throw holiday rotas out of balance. For similar reasons I chose the same time and for many years after that I was to meet him on his way to or from his usual creek and while we never grew close, we would always exchange a few words, usually ones of commiseration. In all the time I knew him he shot nothing, for cruel fate caused the geese to pass him by on either side or miles out of range above his head. He chanced the odd shot but he was no great marksman and he returned home at the end of his six days with nothing to show. In silence he endured the jests of wife, children and colleagues.

Next year he would be back with hope rekindled. Once I noticed he had bought a new gun, a mighty 10-bore which would, he explained, give him a few extra yards of range and bag him a goose from the skeins which flew tantalisingly wide of him. Even this improved fire-power was not the answer and at the end of the week I found myself once more commiserating with him. 'Never mind', he said. 'Better luck next year. I'm determined to bag one of those damn things before they carry me out.'

No less than fourteen years later did success come to George. He had driven thousands of weary miles, spent funds he could ill afford, suffered in moderate lodgings and shivered through four-teen Scottish Januaries, not to mention the taunts of those at home. The lure of the geese was proof against them all, and one day he would bring home his bird to be oft-photographed with him clutching it by the neck, then he would eat it with ceremony and only then might his goose fever subside, the ghost be laid, the mockers silenced.

It was the last day of his week some time in the mid-1970s when snow lay meanly on the Solway sward, Griffel blushed shyly in the sunrise and a skimpy wind swept in from the sea which hissed on the sand half a mile away. As usual the great goose army had gone thundering over, bugles blowing, a mile wide and high as a church and we thought that that was it. However, as so often happens, a smaller skein left out on the sand came in late, beating on, steady as a constellation over the very place I knew George was crouching.

It seemed they had passed him by but then came the distant pop pop of two shots. One goose at the end of the skein lurched and separated, planing off to glide down far behind on the crab grass. George was out of his hide like a sprinter off the blocks. I could imagine his feelings at a fourteen-year wait over but the bird was still not in the bag. George was running like a redshank, game bag flapping about his ears. He had no dog, for his wife would have drawn the line at a muddy spaniel on her best carpets.

It was a stern chase, for the bird was lightly touched. There was some dodging and doubling at the end, but suddenly he flung himself triumphantly headlong on the mud and he had it. I could

see the distant figure plodding back, the precious burden safely cradled. My heart went out to the old boy, success at last and well earned.

I wandered over to share his delight for the flight was over. I reached his hole and was surprised at what I saw, though knowing fowling and fowlers I should not have been. The sight did little to explain the illogical madness of wildfowling, the crazy relationship between hunter and hunted which those opposed to field sports can never understand.

George had taken off his Solway smock baring his shirt to the searing wind. His hat was gone and he was still gasping from the unaccustomed exercise. Carefully wrapped up his coat, its head and neck snaking out, brown eyes unafraid, was a large and lively pink-footed goose. With its beak it plucked tetchily at his sleeve. George looked round, the light of utter exhilaration gleaming from his muddy glasses. He spoke though chattering teeth as gently he stroked the grey feathers. 'It's only wingtipped – hardly touched. I think it can be saved. Is there a vet in the village?'

There was a similar story with a less happy ending, or not, depending on how you look at things, going the rounds on the east coast some years earlier. The Wash marshes were once beloved of the overwintering grey geese, then they deserted it but lately they returned. In the old days, before professional guides and wildfowling clubs adopted the best marshes, it was free for all and one of the most enthusiastic goose hunters was the old Major. Like George his shooting was dogged with ill luck and like George he was to get his goose in the end.

The old fellow had been in military service in India. There he had shot, speared or fished everything that flew, ran or swam. He was the archetypal old shikaree and his adventures with mahseer, pig, tiger and leopard were legendary and faded trophies gazed resentfully down at him from the walls of his gunroom. He had been an avid pig-sticker competing in the Kedhir Cup.

Once on his way home he dismounted from his pony and took a rest on an ant hill. From a bush at his side came a tiny rustle. He prodded the spot with the butt of his spear and a leopard bounded out over him and away. As it passed it lightly dabbed one of its paws on the top if his head. Ever after the old man delighted in lifting a lock of grizzled hair to reveal the long white scar.

In time the old shikaree returned to his native land and settled down with his son Bill to farm a few acres inland of the Wash. There were no tigers or buffalo in Lincolnshire and the village constable's eyes started from his head when he came to inspect the formidable armoury the Major had brought back with him. He took to wildfowling and, being an old hand, soon learned the tricks, discovered the flight lines and bagged his share of wigeon, mallard and teal. He was out most mornings when conditions were right, happily plastered in mud, his red face and bright eyes, which spoke more of whisky than the gymnasium, beaming enthusiasm.

The grey geese eluded him however. Each year it was the same. For a hunter of such prowess it came hard to be defeated by a simple bird but he could never seem to score. Sometimes he came close. Once a family party approached suicidally to where he lay hidden. He was about to rise to shoot when a distant pop pop from the end of the field where another fowler lurked made the birds flare and pass him by. Once he used all his fieldcraft to belly up to a feeding gaggle on a stubble. Again he was 10 yards short when a passing peregrine stooped playfully and put them up. Another time it was a low-flying aircraft.

Most annoying of all was when, gooseless as usual, the Major was plodding off the marsh one morning. There came a low croak from behind him and there were a dozen geese no more than 20 yards up and coming straight over his head. His gun was unloaded and his frenzied clutch at his cartridge bag was far too late. They saw his movement and were gone. 'You know Bill', he said to his son on the drive home. 'I'm never going to get one of those blasted things.'

Seasons became a decade and the Major aged. The doctor gave him dire warnings to take things more easy, 'Dicky heart y' know'. His breath was short, his waistline thickening and legs stiff but still the geese came and still he hunted them. He was well-armed, determined, a good shot and knowledgeable, but somehow…

It happened on Boxing Day just when he least expected it. He was easing himself stiffly out of his favourite creek after another blank with the geese high and handsome. As he rose there came a soft 'wink-wink' from the sea and a skein of about twenty pinks well within range came in from the tide, as often they will after the gunners have gone home for breakfast.

The Major froze in mid-stretch, screwed round his neck at an impossible angle, took in the scene and swung his double 8-bore without moving his feet as he should. He aimed at the leader but the birds were further away than he had thought, for the third bird in line staggered, recovered for a moment, separated from the rest and flew feebly back towards the sea, losing height.

The old fellow was out of his creek and after it, his breath coming in hammering rasps, his heart pounding. There – the bird was down, out on the mud but not dead for it set off running for the sea. The Major fired at it but too far: the shot pattered feebly round it. The bird scuttled and the Major stumbled on, his feet heavy in the clinging mud. Where the devil was that boy with the damned dog? He put on a spurt, the goose always that tantalising 80 yards ahead. Then for some reason it seemed to lose heart for it stopped and crouched in the lee of a miniature cliff of mud. Had it but run on to the sea it would have escaped.

The Major stopped, calmed his hammering heart took aim and fired. The goose sprawled stone dead. A minute later the Major stood gasping but triumphant, a fine old pink-foot gander swinging from its paddles. Slowly he turned and plodded back.

His son Bill grew tired of waiting for the old man back at the meeting place. He retraced his steps down from the sea wall and saw far off the familiar, hunched figure sitting leaning back on a tussock. The defiant, bristling moustache, that incredible hat and long-barrelled gun propped across wadered knees were unmistakable, but what was that in the grass at his feet? Even that far off Bill could distinguish the grey and white of a goose laid out ceremoniously, the mud washed carefully from its feathers.

He gave a war whoop of delight and broke into a run rehearsing the praise he was to lavish on the old fellow. The Major's face wore a smile of beatific content but he said nothing. Words would have been unnecessary as well as impossible and as Bill came panting up his cries of congratulation died on his lips.

The old Major was quite dead.

The Scythe

Down on the marsh there is a man with a scythe. Pause and watch him awhile and marvel at a skill once common but now rare. Draw near and realise that he is not as old as you thought, but one of those ageless men who seem to stop at about fifty and remain the same for ever. He is thin as an old heron, collarless flannel shirt open to the wind, greasy black waistcoat buttoned up. His arms are long and sinewy, on the undersides as snowy-white as the belly of a fish, with a delta of blue veins running down them. On a tussock near the dyke lie his jacket and a bag containing his 'dockey'.

His action is easy, up with the scythe and down, a slight pivoting from the hips and roll of the shoulders, half a step forward and again up, down, a swathe of Norfolk reed falling with a dry sigh to lie ready for the gatherer. Ask him, if you feel so bold, if you might have a try. He is happy to take a break and roll one of his thin cigarettes from the 'makings' in a battered tin and watch for a while. You take up the scythe, it is heavier than you imagined and unwieldy. How could the old folk in the harvest field have swung such a tool for hour after hour of a livelong summer day?

You raise it above your shoulder and bring it down with a mighty swoosh. A swathe of reed falls but somehow the blade binds in the debris and does not come out as when the man did it. You haul it out and have another go, taking in too much this time so that the scythe slows and stops halfway through your cut. You pull it out and hack at the piece you missed. The answer must be more effort so you really put your back into it. Already the sweat is running down your forehead and there is a niggling ache in your back and shoulders. Somehow your cut reed does not lie neatly like his but in a higgledy-piggledy jumble of cut stalks.

After ten minutes you have travelled five yards and have had

enough. You turn to survey your handiwork and see here and there lone sentinels of single reeds you missed standing defiant amid the destruction of their fellows. You hand the scythe back to the man and thank him for his indulgence: there is a new respect in your eyes. He gives a slow smile and takes it. From his belt he takes his rubstone and, laying his leg across the curved handle to brace it, he whets the blade with a clang and a whine of tortured metal which sets your teeth on edge.

Then he is back to work, easy and unstressed, letting the tool work for him, keeping a rhythm which he can maintain all day. He never takes too much at a time nor wastes his energy, common mistakes with beginners. Just a modest swathe, as much as he can encompass without stretching after his half shuffle forward between strokes. His scythe handle has on it a stiff stick which strokes the reed away from him as he swings and causes the cut stalks to lie in orderly fashion, the easier to gather later. Why did it not work thus for you?

He works ankle deep in water. Outside his riverside cottage is a stick stuck in at the water's edge. On a cutting morning he inspects this stick which tells him the level of the river, whether it has risen or fallen during the night. If the stick shows an inch or two deeper he goes to the upstream marsh; if the river has fallen he can work further down. He does not mind working in shallow water but when it is up to his calves he cannot manage.

Most of the reed today is contracted by a local thatching firm. It is cut and bundled by machine in quarter of the time it took in the old days when it was done by hand. The man had to admit that the new method was quick and clean and saved much labour but old habits die hard and he liked to keep his hand in. He had three small beds which he hired and he needed 200 bundles to rethatch his pigsty.

Pass that way again a week later and you might catch him making his bundles in the old way. He has an open coffin on four legs standing at his side and in his hand a comb, a bolt of hickory with four 6 inch nails through it. Taking a bundle of cut reed loosely over his left arm, he combs with vigorous strokes the cut ends, taking out the dead grass and broken stems until the bundle rattles drily in his grasp. He bangs the bundle hard onto a wooden board lying at his feet, combs some more, bangs it again until all the cut ends lie level.

He heaps cut armfuls in his coffin until it is full, removing last minute rogues and tapping the odd loose end into the box. His string is already lying in place across the bottom under the bundle, the traditional 14 inch from the end, and taking it over the top he ties the ancient reed-cutters' knot, pulling it tight so that not even a fingernail could be forced between string and reeds. He makes off his knot with a half-hitch, gives two more vigorous bangs on his board and there is his bundle. A good one is so level at the bottom that on a still day it stands up on its own. He tosses it onto the growing stack at his side.

When he has done he poles over in his punt and stacks the bundles on board. With a good load it looks from a distance like a floating mountain of reeds for the boat has so little freeboard that it seems to vanish beneath the ripples. He poles downstream to his cottage and offloads, making a stack on the bank. Then, a dozen at a time on a flat barrow, he takes the bundles up to his cottage and round the back where they will be needed.

He is the first to admit that his thatching skills are not of the best but working up his ladder he combs and strokes the tough stems into place, pegging, stitching and nailing, shaving the ends until they lie true. The ridge on top cannot be sealed with the stiff reed. It needs fen sedge and he cuts a few bundles, drags it up on a rope and makes a neat line of it, well stitched in to seal the roof and bind over the thatch proper. As a final gesture he fashions a full-sized pheasant out of straw and this he attaches to the end.

The ground round the pigsty is ankle deep in a litter of broken reed and sedge so he rakes it up and heaps it in the yard where he sets a match to it, making sure the wind lies away from his newly finished thatching. The job is done.

If you were privileged or had the time to have dropped in on him during these operations you would feel pleased for him and not a little envious, for such a task from beginning to end would have been beyond you. It called upon skills known to the Saxons and little changed since their day. As for the man, he stands back, rolling another smoke and gazing critically at his handiwork. Slightly rough at this end, perhaps, and a few loose bits over there but not a bad job for an amateur and it would keep his pigs dry. Not only that but it had cost him nothing. The job would, he reflected wryly as he turned away, 'see me out'.

Harmonious Blacksmith

His anvil is silent: the hammer that rang out the rhythms of the changing year is laid aside. With the passing of Walter the blacksmith his business went with him to the grave. People no longer needed his skills and apart from fitting a spade handle, welding a broken mower or a set of fire-irons there had been little work. He tried his hand at wrought iron gates. 'There's good money in them', they told him, but he never settled to that new-fangled business with its delicate bends and curlicues. He preferred something he could get his teeth into.

In his last years his smithy was more than a workshop. Standing at a junction of the two streets in the village it had become a gathering place for the old timers. Thrown out from under the feet of womenfolk keen to get on with housework, they came to the warmth of his glowing coke and sat in a gnarled row on a settle. Half a dozen of them in a bunch represented the accumulated wisdom and village gossip of 500 years. Like a parliament of old rooks or a row of cormorants on a breakwater, they sat hunched, their walking sticks clutched before them, full of wicked slander and homespun philosophy.

Walter would haul on the long handle of his bellows and the fire glowed red, sparks flying up the chimney. Taking in his tongs a bar of metal which glowed cherry-red, he set it on the anvil and gave it a few desultory taps, listening to the talk and making interjections of his own. He was forging hooks for hanging baskets, not his favourite job, but he always said that if it came in iron or steel he could make it.

His forge and the small yard outside were piled high with old iron work. Rusty red in the nettles stood skeletons of cultivators and mangold choppers, antiques when The Old Queen was on the throne, cannibalised long ago to make something else. Tangled

among them were twisted spades, horse chains, plough shares and iron buckets. Inside, rows of horseshoes hung along a rail and in the corner was a pile of scrap-iron of every shape and size awaiting its hour. Ask him for a piece for a particular job and he would bend down and rummage about with much clanging and banging and when he straightened his back he had just the right bit in his hand.

He had time to stop and gossip between hammer blows, but it was not always so. Once he had been busy all day and often well into the evening. Horses stood in a patient queue awaiting shoeing. He was a big, shambling man but the animals felt at ease with him, recognising in him a kindred spirit. In his leather apron he would bend over, a great hairy hoof gripped in the vice that was his knees, and tap and hammer so fast that it bewildered the eye. He would turn with the shoe, heat and hammer it a shade here, a touch there and dip it hissing into the water, offer it up again and nail it on. He shoed them all from the great shires of the farm to the butcher's pony and the horses of the young ladies up at the hall. All came to Walter and would not have dreamed of going anywhere else.

In his prime he could lift his anvil clear off the ground and walk across his yard with it, the mass of metal welded to his leathery hands. It took two men of normal strength to raise it. In time he learned sense and decided not to strain even his massive frame with such unnecessary feats, even when the bet was for a quart of ale. He enjoyed testing his mettle with heavy objects and would hold the beam of a plough with one hand while he hammered a repair. Many a time he made and fitted a new steel rim for a wooden cartwheel, making his circular fire of turves in the yard in the way it had been done since the Romans.

As is often the case with large men he could do the most delicate work if needed. He made an altar rail for the church, bending, tapping and twisting the malleable steel until it was a delicate filigree of leaves and birds with a copper rose in each panel.

Time passed and horses gave way to tractors. He mended more machines but missed the old work. Then came bolt-on technology and new tackle on farms which even he could no longer repair. Finally he was reduced to shoeing the occasional pony for a schoolgirl, putting handles on forks and hoes, making sets of wrought-iron hooks and sometimes a garden gate.

He accepted the changes gracefully for he was a philosophical man. It was the sunset of his years and Walter no longer could boss the foot of a shire horse or swing his greatest hammer.

He was content to potter about with small jobs, 'keeping meself out o' mischief', as he put it. His life had been one of honest toil, contributing to the life of his little community. He was a lusty singer of hymns in church on Sunday and many folk came to him for a quiet word of advice. Here it was a failing crop, there a marriage in difficulty, a wayward son, an unsympathetic bank manager or a pregnant daughter. To all Walter gave his grave ear, his comfort and advice, but kept his own counsel for he was the soul of discretion. A man who was patient with the hard realities of red-hot iron and kicking cart horses found the tribulations of his fellow man minor matters.

Finally his smithy became the parliament of village ancients while he did his pottering, his work habit hard to break. They sat, talked and put the world to rights until it was time to slip across to the pub for a pint of bitter at lunchtime.

This giant of a man died in his sleep in his late seventies. He never retired but saw out an era when agriculture moved from horse to high technology. His trade diminished from the days when he employed a helper and two boys, to the time when all there was to do was tinker.

Now his fire is out, his bellows slack, the ringing of his great hammer, which gave villagers the comfort of knowing that Walter was about his work, is silent. His forge is locked and quiet; a mouse scurries through the sooty dust, past heaps of iron rusting quietly. They lie there still.

As for the old timers, they have nowhere to go in their lonely mornings, and every day the wind blows colder about them without the fire of Walter's furnace and his great heart to warm their ageing bones.

The Poacher's Tale

He sits in the ingle near the log fire which never goes out in the 'snug' bar of the Hare and Hounds. His corduroys have seen better days as have his hob-nailed boots of antique style while his greasy cloth cap is jammed well down round his ears. There are those who have known him for forty years and never seen him bare-headed. His layers of oft-darned woolly jumpers have the hue of old lichen as does his tweed coat, a fugitive from a better wardrobe, which shows many a leather patch.

His face is brown and wizened, his look furtive and darting, never staring at you for long. Avoiding your direct gaze, his eyes swivel sideways at real or imagined events in the far corner of the room. In a crowd he is invisible: in an assembly of three people you would overlook him for somehow, chameleon-like, he fades into any background, saying little but seeming to take in all he sees and hears. If he should deign to shake your hand it will be with a knotty claw, blue-veined and knob-knuckled with arthritis, the fingernails like yellow curds cut from a wax candle. When he moves it is stiffly, his joints thickened after sixty years of kneeling in wet grass and muddy gateways.

In hushed tones, in case he might hear, the locals point him out to visitors, a notorious poacher, an icon of times past and a spokesman of years far removed from the computer screen which rules today. It is like having one of the Krays in your local so you may bask in his reflected glory. This notoriety has earned the old man many a pint from the 'town trade' who drop in on a Sunday evening. They ask him much, he tells them little, doling out the old yarns grudgingly, no wasted words, a deliberate playing down of the deeds of his wild youth and, truth to tell, his equally wild middle-age.

Christened Ezekiel but known from his birthday as Zeke, he was the fifth child in a family of nine, cramped into a three-bedroomed cottage. His father did part-time farm work as the seasons dictated and his mother her best to feed and clothe her hungry brood. As for clothes, it was a case of hand-me-downs and first-up-best-dressed. Zeke was rarely on his bench at the Dame school down the lane but out running wild as a deer along the stream or down by the wood. From his childhood he had an affinity with the woods and fields, seeing 'on the hoof' the food his family so badly needed. The usual home fare was a boiled turnip, stewed nettles and, on high days when his luck was in, the old man might come home with a sheep's head which was a real feast.

While the family went hungry, rabbits, hares and partridges from the great estate swarmed. Conies hopped indolently on the verges, the pheasants roosted big and black in the roadside thorns aware of their immunity from all save the squire's shooting guests and enjoying the protection of a small army of gamekeepers.

A likely lad like Zeke soon learned that a couple of strands of twisted brass wire made a snare and if you set it in the right place at the right height in one of the runs which wound through the grass you might just catch a rabbit. First he brought one rabbit home, then a couple and one early morning he staggered up to the back door of the cottage burdened down with five of them threaded on a stick – no mean load for a skinny lad of eleven.

His parents were grateful for the food and took care that the skins and bones were carefully burned and the innards buried. However, they knew that a keeper had only to catch Zeke in the act and it could mean no more work for the old man and possibly eviction from their tied cottage which belonged to the squire. Zeke took care to cover his tracks leaving no fleck of fur to show where a rabbit had struggled and stroking down the grass so that all looked natural. When he sold a rabbit for a shilling he was careful to let it go only to someone he knew he could trust. Thus was the poacher born to a way of life he was to follow for the next half century.

He preferred rabbits and hares to lordly pheasants: they were all right for the gentry or to sell but not grub for poor men to eat. A good hare could feed a great many people and unless a nosy keeper came sniffing round the back door and caught the aroma of rich gravy it was anonymous enough. A pheasant was more risky: it might flutter off wounded and all those feathers were difficult to hide.

A neighbour had once bagged a pheasant, knocking it down with a well-aimed stick as it strutted among the cabbages in his garden. He sought to hide the evidence by plucking it directly into the kitchen fire. The feathers flew up the chimney in the draught and covered the garden and hedge beyond and before long the keeper was knocking on the door. Another had been reported by a malicious old biddy up the street who told the keeper that her cat was 'allus bringing thim old hare's bones from next door's ash tip'. You had to be careful and know your friends. Even 'Spindle', the village schoolmaster for whom they all had a healthy loathing, sneaked to the keepers of a boy who brought sandwiches with game meat in them for his school lunch.

For all his care and artfulness even Zeke was not immune. Once he had the bad luck to fall off his bicycle right at the feet of an underkeeper and a rabbit slipped from beneath his coat. Another time old Grimes, the head man, stumbled on one of his snares and placed a dead hare in it. Then he lay in wait behind the hedge and leaped on Zeke as he stooped to remove the booty. It was diamond cut diamond and keepers, often reformed poachers themselves, were up to all the tricks. In his youth Zeke escaped with nothing more than a thick ear from keeper or village bobby and once a good whacking with a stick when two keepers bumped into him with a snare trailing from his pocket. In later life he was to be a regular attender in the dock at the magistrate's court.

He graduated from the snare to the long net, a way of taking many more rabbits in a shorter time with no more risk. For this he took his poaching mate, a lad named Joe, as reprobate as himself. The net was cunningly set along the field edge on a windy night. By then the pair had a 'silent dog', necessary for many poaching operations, a brindled lurcher trained to start but not pursue the rabbits. The dog ranged far out on the stubble and the rabbits came striffing through, back to the safety of their burrows. They did not see the net but crashed into it, furry brown balls which

struggled a moment and lay still. Steel fingers felt for neck muscles, each rabbit quivered once and was dead. On their best night they took forty-nine rabbits and sold the lot before the sun was up.

Zeke took hares by setting snares in their runs where they passed through the hedge – 'smeuses' he called these well-worn tracks. The silent dog would quarter the moonlit field, start the hare and 'puss' would streak through her familiar escape route, give a squeal and a kick and lie still. Sometimes the dog would pick one up on his own and come trotting back with it. He was trained to run off home when he heard Zeke whistle so if the keeper caught him and he was ordered to call up his dog, he could whistle until blue knowing that the silent dog would be loping back to the safety of his kennel.

Sometimes he hung a net from a gate knowing that hares will make for a gateway when pursued. Sadly for the silent dog he became even more silent than usual when he ran past the keeper one evening with a leveret in his mouth and the keeper shot him dead. Zeke always mourned the passing of what was his best poaching dog with never another to match it.

Pheasants he shot where they roosted in the thorns. He chose a black and windy night so the pop of the .410 shots would be carried away. Many a time keepers came after him and he learned that it was better to lie low than run away, crashing through the bushes. The keeper was not above firing a random shot waist-high in the general direction of such sounds. Standing silently by a tree-trunk on a dark night he had had a keeper so close that Zeke could smell the pipe tobacco on his coat and still he remained undetected. Other times he lay on his belly like an old fox in the bracken and never was he found. He noted the trees with roosting birds and marked them with a blob of white chalk so that he shot his way back home rather than deeper into enemy territory.

He learned the tricks of the trail netter. Joe would hold the pole at one end of a net twice the size of a double bed sheet, and Zeke the other. The trailing edge weighed down with fishing weights trickled along the stubble. By the time the roosting partridges realised what was happening the net was upon them. Often a whole roosting covey would be taken in this way. This worked well in sugar beet and turnips but the keeper who suspected trail netting would leave clumps of bramble in his best fields so that the fine mesh would tangle and scupper them.

There were setbacks and they did not have it all their own way. Once they were caught red-handed leaving a field with a sack of rabbits and bundle of nets. The keepers believed in rough justice and although they put up stout resistance they were outnumbered and hampered by their gear. They suffered a good thrashing before being hauled down to the police station. The magistrate, himself an estate owner and shooting guest of the squire, had little sympathy for poachers. Thirty days each they got, for the keepers made much of their own injuries: a century before they might well have been deported to the colonies. Fines and short spells in prison mounted up but the art was in their blood and they could no sooner abandon their old ways than a cockerel could resist crowing to the dawn.

Those were the bad old days of the hungry 1930s and during the war that followed most of the keepers were called up, so Zeke had the field to himself and game was in demand. For all his lawlessness he took a perverse pride in his work. He had nothing but contempt for the armed gangs who came from the town, who were short on skills, as they were long on brutality, who cleared a man's coverts in a night and when confronted would think little of shooting down a keeper brave enough to stand in their way. Zeke considered such no better than vermin to be despised, for they brought into disrepute his own skills, in which he took pride, and his ancient and revered craft of the poacher. Not all shared his view, for all poachers were frowned upon by the gentry who made the game laws to protect their precious birds and sat on the bench in judgement of transgressors.

A lifetime of waiting and watching in all weathers had ruined his joints which now were twisted and gnarled as a knotty oak. He cut squares of carpet to tie on the knees of his corduroys but they came too late to do any good. He had learned much by quiet watching. He knew that a feeding deer which constantly stopped to glance behind it meant something or someone was back in the wood. He knew that pigeons clattering from a distant stand of ash poles indicated the approach of a human. He knew the wind, could not read a book but read signs in the dew, invisible to more learned men, which told of the passage of the birds and beasts of the night. He could blend with a hedge in his fustian, ragged clothing so that he seemed to be a part of Nature and not an intruder. He had little time for the shrill noise and clamour of the new age.

Now he sits there in the corner, accepting a pint of old and mild from a stranger, darting his weasel eyes here and there to see who might be listening. 'Best respects' he says raising the glass. He has no need to poach any more for fat times have come to him with his pension and a supermarket down the road. However, the old lust remains, the fire burns as brightly as ever.

He will not let you touch his walking stick but should it ever slip from his fingers and should you chance, politely, to pick it up you will find it surprisingly heavy. Examine it closely, remove the ferrule and there is the muzzle of a gun barrel. Look beneath the handle and spot the rudimentary trigger, for his harmless stick, an old man's prop, is no more than a .410 shotgun cunningly disguised.

He never knows – he might see a pheasant in a bush on his way home from the pub.

Falcon Gentle

In all other respects it was just an ordinary Saturday at the end of January. The ground rang iron-hard after a week of frost and the rusty cutlass blades of dry sedge clashed and rattled in the dykes which themselves lay like silver swords across the black velvet of the peat. Apart from the mean streak of the wind the only other sound that morning was the faint tinkle of a bell. It was no ordinary bell but one fashioned in distant Pakistan from the finest wafer of hammered brass and it was fastened with a leather thong onto the leg of a peregrine falcon.

The art of hunting with hawks – for the ancients termed it more a great art than sport – goes back beyond the dim mists of medieval England. Long before the invention of gunpowder, when even the crossbow was a glint in an armourer's eye, raptors had been trained to hunt not for themselves but for their masters. The yeoman had his short-winged goshawk, that murderous sprinter, an assassin with a marigold, staring eye, working in enclosed spaces through forest glades and round the boles of trees, steering by means of its long train. This bird was death to rabbits and could take a partridge or a mallard sprung from a wet ditch. Its smaller cousin the sparrowhawk was for a priest while the lowliest one of all, the kestrel, was for a knave. The more lordly long-winged falcons were reserved for the aristocracy. In medieval England everything had its place and order.

The manning of a hawk was a challenge for the most patient, for the *Falconidae* are the wildest of birds, top of the food chain, as likely to die through stubbornness as concede to a harsh master. They cannot be broken as a mule or a dog but at best might accept armed neutrality, an uncertain partnership with the falconer. They need sensitive and intelligent handling. Their furniture of hood, leash, jesses and bells are as they always were, tied in place with knots which Uther Pendragon would have recognised. The lore and language of the sport has also changed little. Austringers and falconers today talk of mews, lure, bind, mantle, full-gorged, waiting-on, haggard, high-stomached, cast off, cadge and throwing up, words which were old falconry terms when James I went kite hawking with a cast of peregrines on Royston Heath.

So the man stood and waited on that windy day, his peregrine sitting hooded on his fist, brooding, lost in some medieval nightmare. The man was not an aristocrat and 500 years ago he would have been cast in the stocks and his bird confiscated as being too noble for his station, but that pecking order had long ago been abandoned. His quarry was wild pheasants which had run and skulked in the deep jungles of the dyke banks and the forgotten little spinneys where in summer adders bask and roe deer step daintily. The traditional peregrine's quarry was heron and red kite and, in their day, great bustards on Salisbury Plain.

Pheasant hunting required a third member of the team. A beautiful pointer sat at heel, a delicate pinto of brown and white patches, soft, liquid eyes and a damp nose which could tell you where a pheasant hid a hundred yards upwind. Man, bird and dog were an ancient combination, trained to a high pitch and sharp set to take a pheasant for the pot in the oldest way of all.

A decision made, a line selected, the man chirruped a brief command to his dog and set off along a hairy, choked dyke, walking into the wind for the better scent. Suddenly given her freedom the pointer set off like an arrow, for this breed is no plodding Labrador or spaniel trained to work close at hand within easy range of the gun. She ranged the wide acres quartering back and forth far ahead, tasting the wind until she picked up a scent.

Then she would freeze on point, body rigid, tail like a poker, nose out straight, telling as clearly as human speech where a covey sat. Bird looked at dog, dog looked at bird each waiting for the other to make a move. The spell broken, the game would be up and away with a clatter, otherwise the dog would hold the birds until they or it died of old age. This was the animal you needed for falconry, a dog which would pin down a pheasant by will power, allowing the peregrine time to gain height and take up a station from where she might make a stoop.

The man walked on, his gloved fist held out, his bird sitting as a graven image, the plumes on its hood nodding in the wind like those of a knight at arms. Within fifteen minutes the dog made her first point. She stood as if carved from bog oak, staring at a clump of bleached white grass with stalks of dead Norfolk reed protruding like a bizarre crown from its top. The point was good: she was solid, thought the man. This was no frog or dead rabbit but a pheasant for sure; he knew by the way she was standing. He removed the hood from his falcon, using his teeth in the old way to loosen the leather thong.

The peregrine stared around arrogantly and roused, twirling her feathers like a mop. The man held his arm out and up, facing her into the wind. In her own time she fell from the wrist, two flaps and she was skimming low across the field, the man shouted, 'Ho Ho Ho!' She turned and banked coming back and making height. She circled above him, each turn higher than the last and up and up she went until that black crossbow shape was etched against the grey sky and the man had to squint and screw up his eyes to see her. This was an anxious moment. From her lofty vantage point she might spy a distant flock of pigeons or plover, for her eyes were a hundred times sharper than his and the call of the wild was still strong within her. If she flew off now she might never return.

The worry faded for back she came, now more than five hundred feet from the ground, her world stretched out below her, a patchwork of fields, the tiny man, the toy dog still on point, a scene she knew well, for she had been trained to expect what was about to happen. She came overhead and slowed down, almost stalling, what falconers know as 'waiting on', holding position in the best place from which to stoop. The man knew that this was 'the time'

and with a shout he leaped down into the grassy knoll where the dog had promised him a pheasant sat. The bird did not flush immediately for it had seen the falcon high above and knew the danger but at last, if only to avoid his tramping boots, a hen pheasant burst forth with a squeak, the white squirt of a dropping and whir of wings and set off low across the corn drill to the safety of the wood on the far side.

She never made it. This was the moment the man had been awaiting. Now came the few electric seconds when the training, the expense, the self-sacrifice and many disappointments all seemed worthwhile. One moment wide-winged and almost hovering, the falcon shrank to a sliver of black and plummeted down. The speed of the stoop has been variously estimated at about one hundred miles an hour but it seems quicker. Like a razor blade slitting the throat of the sky she sliced and twisted through the heavens so fast that the man could hear the shrill whine of the wind through her leather jesses which streamed out straight behind her.

Judging the moment to perfection peregrine and pheasant met, the gap between them closing like the onrush of Armageddon from which there was no escape. The falcon struck with the sound of a stick hitting a bag of wet cement. There was a squirt of brown feathers, the falcon bound on with the terrible grip of scimitar talons and both birds crashed to the ground with another stream of feathers blowing pale against the sooty earth. The hairs on the back of the man's neck never failed to prickle at the sight which he held to be the most thrilling spectacle in Nature.

Then he was across the dyke and running over the field to where his falcon sat on its victim, her wings mantled to protect it from thieves, tearing out beakfuls of feathers. The man approached the last few paces cautiously. He did not wish to wrest the quarry away from his bird and thus make her less keen to hunt. He offered her a tasty morsel of food and in time she left her kill and tore to shreds the scrap in his fingers. Had she gorged her fill on the pheasant she would not hunt again that day.

He tucked the pheasant into his bag, called up his dog and set off again along the reedy dykes. His next adventure was similar in build-up and again the falcon waited on perfectly. This time the game was up and away too soon, a large cock pheasant strong on the wing and weighing more than twice as much as its adversary. Again came the heart-stopping stoop, again the smack and puff of feathers but this time the grip was less sure, the pheasant recovered its equilibrium and flew on, diving into the protecting willow stubs, giving a double crow of triumph as it did so. Had it possessed fingers instead of feathers it would have raised two of them in defiance.

Next his falcon was lured away by a passing pigeon. With a double flick of its wings and wind assisted it was two fields away and still going. The man whirled his feathered lure and shouted but in vain. One thing he had which the ancients did not was a telemetry device. There was a tiny transmitter fastened to the root of the falcon's tail while the man carried an aerial and receiver in his bag. Following the electronic blip, he made a beeline across the ploughing and half a mile away he found the falcon sitting on a dead tree. She came down straight away to the morsel of food on the lure.

He killed one more pheasant before the sour-lemon sun slid behind the poplars which marked the farm boundary. He would have many days worse than this, days when it rained, when his bird flew off, when the dog was unsteady or there was no game, but today he had no complaints. He allowed the falcon to feed her fill on the last pheasant, for he knew that they were done for the day. She tore it to shreds with awesome power and then, her crop bulging, full gorged and hooded once more, her head sank into her shoulders and she lapsed into her murderous dreams.

Whistling up his dog and shortening his bag strap for the long walk home, he sought out the nearest footpath and set off briskly, back to where he thought he had left his car.

Bats in the Belfry

The bell-ringers were at it again. Far beyond the village, sweetened by distance, filtered through summer trees, its hard edge taken off by acres of standing corn, the sound drifted to the ears of those working in the fields. Folk with babies who needed their sleep and who lived in the shadow of the church were not so charitable, for there was no escape from that wild music which might well last for two hours on a practice night.

The church had what campanologists know as a 'ring' of six bells with a tenor in E which weighed in at the best part of a ton. They had been cast long ago by those doyens of bell founders, Taylors of Loughborough who had only the Whitechapel foundry in London as rivals in their ancient craft.

The bells hung and swung high above the west end of the church and had marked with their brazen shouts great occasions, national and local triumphs and disasters – the Battle of Waterloo, the ending of the Great War and its successor the Second World War, countless weddings and the rising of great floods which drowned the low-lying acres. Then the bells called the folk up the hill to sanctuary. 'Awake! Awake! Fire, Foes, Floods! Awake!' They came grey with fatigue clutching their few possessions, children whimpering at heel, dogs, cats and even a pig in tow. Their cottages stood bedroom-deep in yellow flood water until, almost gently they crumbled, slipped and fell into the tide for their foundations were on peat and silt. The church was full of refugees drinking hot soup, their animals tethered to gravestones outside, all wondering what the future held for them.

Sometimes the sonorous tenor bell would toll alone to mark the passing of a villager, the right number of strokes for man or woman and one for every year of their lives. Those harkening as they worked in the fields were reminded of their own mortality by this dolorous sound. 'Ask not for whom the bell tolls…it tolls for thee. . .'

More cheerfully in piping times of peace the bell-ringers went tramping up the eighty stone steps to the ringing chamber, took off their jackets and spat on their hands. The door to the tower was low and narrow, made for smaller folk of the fourteenth century. We had to stoop to get through it and then wind up the spiral steps, each one worn in the middle where countless feet long gone had trod that way before. Gasping for breath we reached the first landing. Through another door hung the bell ropes, their fluffy sallies tricked out in red, white and blue stripes, each rope made off neatly with a half-hitch.

The smell was of chalky dust, old hassocks, a hint of mice and something else which could have been bats for there was a colony of pipistrelles high above in the spire. Our jackets hung in a row on brass hooks. I would clamber up onto the window ledge, eight feet wide so stout were the walls, and peer down through the leaded panes at the street below, the postman like a crawling ant going from door to door and a miniature tractor out on a field making neat stripes of paler colour as it toiled back and forth.

Then it was to work. As not only a beginner but the boy I took the smallest treble bell. The old hands spread themselves around. Claude always liked to ring number four, old Sam liked the tenor. Gimbert, Feast, Few, Faux, Murfitt – the old village names were there, hands on the sallies waiting. 'A little touch of Plain Bob', barked the conductor. Then came my one great moment for I had to start the whole thing off. 'Treble's going: she's gone', I piped and gently pulling my rope the bell rolled over, past the vertical, off balance and round she swung, pivoting back and up. In succession the next five ropes snaked down and flew up to the ceiling, whipping through the pulley holes and back down again. Pause, watch the bell which rang before yours, wait your turn, gently pull, and up again.

We started with rounds, 1, 2, 3, 4, 5, 6 trying to keep the rhythm even and then at the signal the bells began to hunt back and forth, passing each other and when the conductor roared 'Bob!', dodging back and weaving through the pattern of sound.

On the treble my job was to hunt back and forth with no complicated manoeuvres which was just as well. When we got into a muddle there was no extricating ourselves. Bells would clash simultaneously, sometimes a long pause and then four bells would strike at once with a hideous cacophony. We stared round wildly, completely lost: where to go next? In the end in desperation the conductor would bellow 'Rounds!', and we would try to return to simple rounds before once more launching off onto uncertain waters. No wonder those living close by were disgruntled.

When it went well it was satisfying and the end of a 'touch', as we called it, was a feeling of triumph. At weddings we would wait for a crate of beer to be sent up, a thing which by no means all wedding parties remembered, in which case we showed our displeasure by ringing for a shorter time. On the good days a man would come staggering in having lugged his crate of light ale up all those stairs.

On the many days when I was a spectator, there being more ringers than bells to go round, I would slip out of the bell chamber and up the next flight of stairs to where the bells hung. The great masses of bronze with their shouting mouths splashed white with owl droppings swung round, up to the vertical, paused and back down again with a noise which seemed to pierce your very skull. With massive bolts they were fastened to rough-hewn trunks of great trees in the form of a frame which straddled the inside of the tower. I had just read *The Nine Tailors* by Dorothy L. Sayers and recalled how, with their racket, the bells had once killed a man imprisoned in the belfry.

Climb the ladder up to the leads, slide up the bolt on the trap-door and creep out onto the top, grip with white knuckles the rough battlements and survey the village below laid out like a map and gaze far off into the misty distances. It was said that you could see forty other church towers from that point on a clear day but I have never spotted more than half that number. The lead of the roof was scratched and scored with many a set of initials, often carved by those on fire watch during the war. It would have been a cold and tedious lookout point during the weary hours of a winter's night.

When the bells were ringing the whole tower rocked gently to and fro. It was amazing to me that those great slabs of Barnack rag could move with so fluid a motion that you could feel a thousand tons of it swinging beneath your feet. Had they not done so the tower would have disintegrated under the power of that mass of metal on the move.

One New Year's Eve we rang a peal, a succession of changes which went on for three-and-a-half hours. It was an adventure, not only a significant 'first' for any bell-ringer but I was allowed to stay up late. Eagerly I clambered up the steps at quarter before midnight with my flask of hot soup and packet of sandwiches. It was Plain Bob Minor when as usual nothing more was required of me than hunting back and forth while the rest of them dodged around me. The turnip watch of our conductor showed the witching hour and we were off. 'Treble's going...'

It went perfectly with no mistakes or even anxious moments. I had heard of a bell-ringer whose braces burst and he completed a peal with his trousers round his ankles but there was not even that for light relief. The shout of the bells floated over the sleeping village and out across the dreaming fields twixt frozen fen and the iron sky, while high above the stars and a new moon as thin as a widow's wedding ring twinkled watchfully in the frost.

At last we were there, safely back at the end of thousands of changes and into rounds again which we enjoyed for a few moments trying to make them as good as we could until at last the conductor called 'Stand'. This meant stop next time and this could be slightly worrying. Pull a mite too hard and the bell struck the kicker and back it bounced for another stroke.

Everyone else stopped and your solitary bell rang out twice more spoiling the effect: they all knew who was the culprit and there were accusing glances. However, even this went smoothly and all at once we stopped, a sudden cessation of sound with just the echoes fading. We tied up our ropes, shook hands, wished each other a Happy New Year and filed down the stairs.

Claude Gimbert who was tower captain came down last having checked that all lights were turned off and with an enormous key he locked the little door. We called our goodnights and tramped off to our beds in the chilly hush of the pre-dawn, proud that we had done our bit to christen the New Year. At the gate of my house I turned and looked back at the dark bulk of the tower, known locally as 'The Pepperbox', where it loomed outlined against the stars. Now it was dark and silent.

One day the sun would shine and the bells would ring again. Younger hands would pull the sallies and worry about the changes long after those who had rung this night lay under grassy mounds in the churchyard beneath. Such venerable bells were no strangers to seeing people come and go: they at least were constant in a world of change.

Hail and Farewell

The village of my youth was very different from the village today. The skeleton remains the same but the flesh has changed. There is the same High Street with lanes running from it like ribs angling from a fish's backbone. Some of the trees survive, thicker in girth, others lost to storms and 'developments', while the church stands four square on the highest point as it has done since the fourteenth century. The changes are all to do with new prosperity, new ways in agriculture and new people.

There are some fine houses in the High Street built by Dutchmen who came to drain the fens in 1630. Small shops had been tacked onto their fronts so we could buy nails, seeds, shotgun cartridges, paraffin, bread, string and galvanised buckets – in other words the essentials. The old village needed to be self-sufficient with its own baker, garage with a hand pump for petrol, wool shop, grocery with a boy who delivered on his bicycle, post office cum toy shop, ironmonger, undertaker and even a little fishing tackle shack. The new mobile villagers with their new money shop at the supermarket six miles away and one by one the fine old houses were renovated. The jerry-built shop extensions which once seemed as permanent as the church itself were knocked down and the original windows and brickwork restored.

Farmyards with scratching hens, a rudimentary pigsty, mouldering ricks and, in the nettles, farm implements which Turnip Townsend would have recognised, became residences for the rich, with tended gardens and double garages, the 'Jag' parked outside and geraniums in hanging baskets.

The street system is bustling with traffic. Once it was so quiet that children would lie down in the middle of the road for a 'dare' for so long that they grew bored waiting for someone to drive along to test their mettle. In the old village there were three cars and later two delivery vans, the sort with the oval windows in the back doors. To exceed 20 miles an hour was to taste life in the fast lane. All other transport was horse and cart or the ubiquitous bicycle.

Where once there were ten pubs now there are three. Beer which cost 1s a pint is now closer to £2 and fast food is yours at a snap of your fingers. The pubs were places of meeting where folk discussed matters of importance, such as the fishing season and the fortunes of the cricket team. High prices have driven away working folk and it is commuters and travellers who prop up the bar and order their scampi and chips with salad on the side. Folk have forgotten how they struggled for survival and wasted nothing. All you need, and much that you do not, is on tap and no longer do villagers need to hunt the hedges for blackberries and nuts and scour the common for mushrooms. Now it is only time which has become precious.

I recall the first television in the village. It was a huge cabinet with a goldfish bowl in the middle. It took some time to warm the valves so you switched on long before you intended to view. The first programme I saw was the Boat Race of about 1955, watched in a curtained room in a reverential hush with the master of the house darting up to adjust vertical or horizontal hold as the picture slipped sideways or down or dissolved into a snowstorm. No one else was permitted to fiddle with the knobs.

Now every house bristles with aerials so you may watch sex and violence every day for twenty-four hours if you wish. Gone are the days when there was one channel and on it long periods of inactivity filled with the potter's wheel or swimming goldfish. Some nights at news time the announcer would appear in his dinner jacket and inform the viewers that there was no news tonight so it was back for another spell at the potter's wheel.

Time was when the cricket team was drawn entirely from villagers, and a fearsome lot they were too. Men iron-hard after lifetimes of digging or ploughing with horses made up for with vigour what they lacked in art. Our most feared player was Herbie Spragg, a red-haired giant of a man who bowled with ferocious pace from a long run up and terrified the batsman into surrendering his wicket. As a youth, fielding somewhere in the deep among tussocks inhabited recently by a herd of cows with loose bowels, I watched with awe as Herbie came thundering up to the wicket to hurl down one of his cannonballs and blessed the fact that he and I were on the same side.

When batting Herbie did not care to be given out for anything less than a clean bowled. When the finger of dismissal was raised for any other reason he would stalk down the wicket and upbraid the umpire. 'That weren't out be a mile – are you blind…?', and nervous men had been known to reverse the verdict. Here was a shade of the greatest batsman of all, W. G. Grace, who when given out by a youthful umpire early in his innings at an exhibition match told him, 'Young man: people have come to see me bat, not you umpire. Kindly reverse your decision'. Without waiting for an answer he stalked back to his crease.

In the football team Herbie was just as much a scourge of referees and one man frightened for his life was said to have fled from the field and leaped onto a passing bus on its way to Ely. He was never seen again and the match continued without him, and good riddance.

At least our teams were home produced. Lanky youths outgrown their strength, men too fat to run, old codgers, raw-boned chaps from the harvest field, the doctor's son and the tradesmen all turned out. The umpiring was done by the schoolmaster, a man not easily intimidated. Today, village cricket is full of folk from away keen to get a game, usually better players than the press-ganged stalwarts of the old days, so the village team ceased to be a village team in all but name. They built a new pavilion, insisted on whites for all players, removed the cowpats from the outfield and even practised. The old days of fun, laughter and uninhibited rivalries had gone for ever.

The bell tower on the village school was truncated and now well-shod children arrive by car and are taught on banks of computers where once it was chalk, a little whippy stick and a solid commitment to the three R's. Gone are the hobnailed boots known as 'sparkies', for by scraping hard on the road the steel hobs on your heels flashed a satisfying squirt of sparks. Now they wear trainers, are well-dressed with no hand-me-downs and prepare for citizenship in tomorrow's world, whatever that might hold.

Where once the shooting was virtually free and a man with a gun and a dog could wander where he wished, avaricious farmers have 'taken in hand' the sporting rights, reared pens full of silly pheasants and sell days to 'furriners'. Even the wild wastes of the Bedford washes which ran along the bottom of the village have become valuable sporting property. Where once I bought land for £35 an acre you would be lucky to get hold of it for £2000. Step over the boundary or attempt to wander as in the old days and look out for trouble.

The stern village policeman, Mr Armstrong, with his military moustache, piercing blue eyes and his bicycle has gone. He was expert at clipping the ears of recalcitrants; this was the man who dealt with my case when I was caught fishing without a licence – fined 10s and don't do it again. He was held in respect and what little trouble we had he handled thanks to his shrewd local knowledge. Law and order are now behind the wheel of a Panda car which makes swift and infrequent sorties through the village. Petty crime is on the increase. Where once you not only left your doors open but folk were welcome to come in and even make a cup of tea when you were out, the new houses sport burglar alarms for all to see under the eaves.

Most of all the people have changed. Stroll past the yew trees and round the churchyard and see on the gravestones a catalogue of the old village names, men who were middle-aged when I was young. They were rabbit catchers, farmers, harvesters, anglers, cricketers, eel catchers and shopkeepers who wrested a living from the ingenious use of the things they found around them. My father and mother lie there too, for they were part of the old ways during and after Hitler's war.

In their place is a new breed, folk from towns who sought out the rural life for reasons best known to themselves. They bought and 'did up' the old cottages and certainly breathed new life into mouldering parochial institutions. They and their children know much of computers and calculators but little of the song of a skylark, the dash of a sparrowhawk or the quiet pools where the tench lie. They cannot tell wheat from barley and have not the need nor the know-how to scrimp and save when winter looms. No doubt they are no better or worse people than those in whose cottages they live but of the old countryside and the ancient rhythm of the seasons they know nothing.

Let cockerels crow too loudly in the mornings, shots be fired near their houses or a cowpat appear in the High Street and they slap on an injunction as sure as harvest. The few old survivors have deserted the land, for where the harvest gangs once toiled twenty-strong, a lone operative on a combine harvester can do it all in a fraction of the time and better.

The constant factor is the church, the ancient tower which rears high above the village, pointing to heaven and overlooking the patchwork of fields and dwarfing the little comings and goings of humans. It has seen it all many times, small aspirations and changes sudden or gradual. Who knows but in another century we will become a peasant community again, having found the technological age lacking the spirituality which every man needs.

That tower has stood for six hundred years as mute witness to the changes wrought to the earth by the Almighty. It will regard as very small beer the changes wrought by Man.

Oft did the harvest to their sickle yield.
Their furrow oft the stubborn glebe has broke:
How jocund did they drive their team afield!
How bow'd the woods before their sturdy stroke!

Let not Ambition mock their useful toil,
Their homely joys, and destiny obscure;
Nor Grandeur hear with a disdainful smile
The short and simple annals of the poor.

from 'Elegy written in a Country Churchyard'
Thomas Gray 1716–1771